St. Louis in Watercolor

The Architecture of a City

by

Marilynne Bradley

With an Introduction by Ron (Johnny Rabbitt) Elz
And a Foreword by Esley Hamilton

REEDY PRESS

St. Louis, Missouri

Reedy Press
PO Box 5131
St. Louis, MO 63139

Library of Congress Control Number: 2008931529

ISBN: 978-1-933370-71-2

Please visit our website at www.reedypress.com.

Printed in China
08 09 10 11 12   5 4 3 2 1

CONTENTS

Preface and Acknowledgments

Since the city was founded in 1764, St. Louis has progressed from a settlement of log houses scattered along the riverfront to an expanding metropolis with the fourth largest population in the nation by 1904.

The community grew under three flags: Spanish, French, and American. A colorful cast of characters passed through its first century: explorers, fur traders, Native Americans, boatmen, immigrants, small shopkeepers, great financiers, manufacturers, and tycoons of commerce.

The heritage of St. Louis is reflected in its magnificant collection of architectural structures. The influences include Egyptian, Greek Revival, Romanesque, Gothic, Art Deco, and more. Often, the buildings are combinations of the various styles.

Every building has a story. Through my brushstrokes I am able to capture these structures in a telling watercolor. The paintings are a collection of forty years of recording St. Louis scenes on paper. My first job, as an architectural illustrator working for Ralph Fournier, introduced me to the heritage of this river city. The fascination of multiple historic examples of St. Louis architecture make for excellent subject matter. This interest in historic scenes has continued.

I gratefully acknowledge the assistance and advice and editing of Matt Heidenry of Reedy Press, Esley Hamilton, and Johnny Rabbitt. I thank Vic Miller, my husband, who helped me assemble my writings in a concise manner. Through his patience, understanding, and companionship, I was able to give full concentration in researching and writing the text. I could devote at any time, day or night, to paint the subject matter of this area with its many firsts west of the Mississippi.

Marilynne Bradley

Foreword

This collection of some of Marilynne Bradley's best watercolors over the past quarter century or more is also a tour of St. Louis as it has looked over that time. Here, we find some of our most familiar landmarks, places with national and even international standing such as the Wainwright Building, the Eads Bridge, and the Arch. We also find places that are treasured by St. Louisans but not so well known elsewhere: the Bird Cage in Forest Park, the Fox Theatre, Soulard Market, and the Bevo Mill, for example. Bradley records the centers of high culture—the art, science, and history museums, Washington University, the two Catholic and one Episcopal cathedrals. And on the flip side, she features one place that has become the quintessential exemplar of popular culture in this region, Ted Drewes' frozen custard stand. All the places that make St. Louis fun to live in seem to be here.

But we also find, with a pang of regret and maybe even with a twinge of resentment against the people who have destroyed them, places that we have loved and lost: popular gathering places, some of high artistic merit, including Edward Durrell Stone's Busch Stadium, the Arena, the *Goldenrod Showboat*, the Parkmoor and the White Castle restaurants; historic landmarks such as the Rock House; and a sampling of the many downtown buildings that have disappeared during this time, the Title Guaranty and Buder Buildings and the unique art glass Egyptian Revival lobby of the Hadley-Dean Building. Set against this, we have such successes as the transformation of Lafayette Square from a risky place frequented only by urban pioneers into one of the most desirable neighborhoods in the city. And the reconstruction of the Grand Basin in Forest Park to evoke the great World's Fair of 1904 has ironically turned out to be one of the best and most appreciated achievements of new design the city has seen for many years.

In these pages we can weigh the city's successes and failures, its joys and sorrows. But we should never forget that while in one sense they document the city's appearance, Marilynne Bradley's watercolors are not simply records. They are works of art, and as such they are able to delve beneath the surface appearance of the world to find the deeper essence of those places and those experiences. The Coral Court Motel, for instance, was one of the region's most controversial landmarks. Known locally for the colorful, even slightly off-color stories that swirled around it, this Art Deco motor court with over thirty separate buildings gradually became nationally recognized as one of the most important examples of roadside architecture of its era and a premiere landmark of Route 66, the Mother Road. By the time it was torn down in 1996, however, it had become a faded shadow of its legendary self. The image of the Coral Court that most of us carry with us is not the sad reality but the sparkling memory captured in Marilynne Bradley's watercolor. Again and again, Marilynne has been able to catch these St. Louis places not just as those of us who love them see them, but as we think of them. Such is the power of art.

Esley Hamilton

Introduction

Over the years there have been countless artists, working in diverse media, and in unique methods, to chronicle the landmarks of the St. Louis area by documenting the look and feel of our wealth of architectural artifacts. A few of the names that come to mind are Roscoe Misselhorn, Siegfried Reinhardt, Norbury Wayman, Bob Shay, Michael Eastman, Orville Spreen, George McCue, William Stage, Scott J. MacNutt, Harry Hagen, Robbi Courtaway, Wayne St. Wayne, Savo Radulovich, Thomas Crone, Joe Bufalo, Candace O'Connor, Jay Landesman, Elizabeth McNulty, Fr. William Barnaby Faherty, S.J., Mary Bagley, Michael Kilfoy, Robert and Eldon Arteaga, Steve De Bellis, Cyril Kolocotronis, Mary Bartley, and James Godwin Scott. Now we submit the name and works of Marilynne Bradley to this fretfully far from complete list of image-makers. If you love our town, you'll be quickly enamored by this effort with its illuminating combination of prose and pictures, examining places that have, and are having, an effect on our quality of life.

There's a strong feeling of continuity with Bradley's fresh, vibrant watercolor images that grace the pages of this book. It's as if we are seeing these mostly familiar sites in a new way, a way that gives promise and hope that this continuum will remain for those who will follow us. With their accompanying concise historical notations, even the places that have passed into oblivion seem to remain vital and uncannily alive. The words related to and the likenesses of the landmarks that have been lost will unfortunately instill a feeling of sadness that these entities, once threads of the fabric of our lives, came unraveled and disappeared. There's the Old Rock House that pre-dated Missouri's statehood. It never did turn its back to the river, as have almost all other places in St. Louis.

In these pages you'll get a glimpse of the exterior of Little Bohemia, the actual international birthplace of the "beat generation" of the post–World War II period. Its full name was Little Bohemia Art Galley Studio Bar, and it was a haven for the creative type. It occupied a spot at 220 S. Fourth Street that was on the first floor of the small, antiquated, downright eerie, Erie Hotel. Little Bohemia opened at the end of Prohibition under ownership of artist Savo Radulovich and the place had an almost magical attraction for artists and writers due to the gregarious Savo and his Bohemian staff that included a well-remembered waitress named Lola Martinovich. There always seemed to be more paintings and drawings filling the walls of Little Bohemia than you'd find at the Art Museum. After the war, Jay Landesman and Ray Dyreks assisted Radulovich in guiding the destiny of this esoteric establishment. In the mid-1950s, Landesman opened his first Crystal Palace club in the 3500 block of Olive St. as somewhat of a spin-off of Little Bohemia. In the late 1950s, Landesman moved lock, stock, and stained-glass to 4236 Olive St. and Gaslight Square. Downtown got a new "beat" hangout with the opening of Frank Moskus' Yacht Club that was moored on the levee south of the *Admiral.* Hmmm, the haunts of The Square and the Yacht Club would be perfect fodder for Marilynne Bradley's brushes. I'll have to mention this to her.

More people will likely read about and see the ill-advised and ill-fated flop, the *Santa Maria,* in this book than actually saw this short-termed faux historical aberration on our riverfront. It possibly would have had some success had it been dismantled and moved to a site adjacent to the von Miller, of Munich, Christopher Columbus statue in Tower Grove Park. This monument presents Columbus as standing on the deck of his *Santa Maria,* and there's a bas-relief on the south side of the George Barnett–designed red granite pedestal depicting the ship's deck at the time of the discovery of America. The ersatz *Santa Maria* fizzled faster than the Toledo Room and the Sir John Falstaff Theatre that had attempted to ignite interest in the Spanish Pavilion.

Then there's Busch Memorial Stadium, that was the intermediary between the north-side Sportsman's Park and our now retro-Busch. Edward Durrell Stone's Busch Stadium was home to the baseball and football Cardinals as well as to the Browns. When the circa 1966 Busch Stadium was being created, it supplanted places such as the Grand Theatre at 514 Market Street that was originally the once grand, Grand Opera House, which became the Grand Opera Playhouse and lastly the Grand Berlesk Theatre. Other spots that struck out to make way for the stadium were the 220-room York Hotel at 8 S. Sixth Street, the popular Asia restaurant at 720 Market Street, the On Leong Chinese Merchants Association at 722 and other flimsy remnants of our St. Louis Chinatown dubbed Hop Alley. Also falling to the wrecking-ball were the nineteenth-century "New" St. Nicholas Hotel and the Herder bookstore both on S. Broadway, as well as St. Louis Wholesale Drug on S. Seventh Street. A very high percentage of the land taken for the stadium had by the mid-1940s become surface parking lots and service stations.

Today, Busch Memorial Stadium is gone, extracted like a not-yet-decayed tooth pulled by an over-zealous dentist. At this writing, the site, which is waiting for the long promised Ballpark Village is a swamp-like, weed-infested, trash-strewn eyesore that resembles either Berlin at the end of World War II or the ravaged property that once held the behemoth and ill-conceived Pruitt-Igoe housing project, which covered several square blocks in the vicinity of Jefferson Boulevard and Cass Avenue. That complex of high-rise tenements was imploded in 1976, and yet today the grounds are literally an urban jungle. The differences are: 1. The old stadium site is in the high-visibility heart of a struggling-to-survive downtown; 2. The property is owned by millionaires. Marilynne, this is not suitable subject matter for your watercolors.

The complex of viable and historic buildings that comprised the block bounded by Seventh and Eighth, Market and Pine streets got in the way of the Gateway Mall plan that was to have allowed for an elongated one-block, wide-open, park-like space from the east side of the Civil Courts building on N. Eleventh Street to the west side of the Old Courthouse on N. Broadway. The principal structures felled were the twelve-story Buder Building and the equally tall Title Guaranty Building. The 1902 Buder, which was a design of William A. Swasey, had been known by other names including Liggett & Meyers. The 1898 Title Guaranty was the work of architects Eames & Young, who also designed the 1914–1920 Marquette Building at 300 N. Broadway; the 1896 Mississippi Trust Building at the northwest corner of Fourth and Pine streets; the Cupples Station buildings bounded by Spruce, Poplar, Seventh, and Eleventh streets, which were erected in 1892; and the 1902–1905 Frisco Lines Building at 906 Olive Street. After the buildings of the Buder/Title Guaranty block were razed, the announced plan of a seven-block open plaza swiftly fell by the wayside and the block was filled with a ho-hum office complex.

The mothballed, one-hundred-year-old (in 2009) *Goldenrod Showboat* was said to have had an interior décor reminiscent of that of the Majestic Theatre in Denver, Colorado. The *Goldenrod* was always plain-Jane on the outside, but inside it had the look of a veritable floating palace. Its original name was *W. R. Markle's New Showboat,* for the boat's owner who was nicknamed "Double R" Markle. Markle had bought his first boat, *Swallow and Markle's Grand Floating Palace,* in 1901 with money he made by card-playing and gambling. Reports of that era indicate that it was "grand," but it paled with respect to the size, superior quality of construction, and decoration of his "New Showboat" of 1909. The *New Showboat* was, at the suggestion of Markle's sister, rechristened as the *Goldenrod*. The *Goldenrod* was unequaled by any other showboat. A special steamboat, called the *W. R. Markle,* was built to tow the engineless *Goldenrod* along the rivers. If you're a fancier of the rivers and the boats that plied them, we strongly suggest a visit to the Pott Inland Waterways Library and Collection that's housed at the Mercantile Library. The Mercantile, no relation to the old Mercantile Bank, is now located adjacent to the Thomas Jefferson Library at the University of Missouri–St. Louis. Metrolink will practically take you to the door.

Meanwhile, back on board the *Goldenrod*, Captain J. William Menke took possession of the theatrical vessel in 1922. He purchased the *Goldenrod*, "The World's Greatest Showboat," from Ralph Emerson, who had owned it since 1914. Fifteen years after Menke took the helm, he brought the boat to St. Louis for repairs with no plans to play for the "city slickers." There was also an ordinance against wooden theatres. He had a change of heart and presented a production of "East Lynne" after getting a federal court ruling that the Mississippi River did not belong to any city, therefore any anti-wooden theatre ordinance was unenforceable. The slickers took to the "mellerdramas" like flies to honey, and Menke was here to stay, performing such classics as "Hamlet & Yeggs," "Lena Rivers," and "Traffic In Souls." Cap'n. Billy lived on the boat itself, and according to later operators, Frank Pierson and John and Ron Auble, his ghost still walks the now-dreary decks. I do believe there's a for-sale sign on the *Goldenrod*, just in case you're interested.

When the Arena, which was originally to be called the Highlands Arena, opened on September 23, 1929, the event was euphoric, as were the times. A promotional brochure described it this way: "Here champions will be made . . . amid the plaudits of 20,000 spectators. Pageantry and the super-spectacle drama, music and the voices of great conclaves will be seen and heard. . . ." Few seemed to know that the economy of our great country would plunge into Depression just over a month later. Things got so bad at the Arena that the hockey team, the Flyers, a Chicago Blackhawk's farm club, on the day after Christmas in 1932 played the only indoor hockey game on natural ice. The Arena had a refrigeration system for a recently installed, and world's largest, indoor ice-hockey playing surface, but the building's owners were unable to pay the electric bill. So they filled the surface with water, opened all the doors and windows, and with the help of Mother Nature, the water froze and the game was played. The Flyers lost. Shortly thereafter the Arena went into foreclosure.

The Arena hosted such acts and teams as Tom Mix, the Three Stooges, Frank Sinatra, Sally Rand, Duncan Renaldo and Leo Carillo as the Cisco Kid and Pancho, the Grateful Dead, Ice Capades, St. Louis Spirits basketball, the Moody Blues, Cole Brothers Circus, St. Louis Braves hockey, the Ice Follies, the Billy Graham Crusade, Luciano Pavorotti, St. Louis Hawks basketball, Billy Joel, Saint Louis University Billikens hockey, the Firemen's Rodeo, St. Louis Blues hockey, the Bee Gees, Sonya

Henie Hollywood Ice Review, Neil Diamond, St. Louis Bombers basketball, Led Zeppelin, St. Louis Steamers soccer. The Arena hosted everything from boxing and tennis, to the Harlem Globetrotters as well as turtle racing.

In addition to the previously noted *Goldenrod, Santa Maria,* and *Yacht Club,* our riverfront was at various times the address for a number of other entertainment boats during the twentieth century. There was *The President;* the *Saint Paul;* the *J. S.;* the *J. S. De Luxe;* the *Inaugural;* a World War II minesweeper; a Burger King floating restaurant; a McDonald's floating restaurant; the *River Queen,* a vintage vessel that housed a restaurant; the reproduction Robert E. Lee restaurant; and of course, the streamlined, stainless-steel SS *Admiral,* which was the extensively remodeled *Albatross* that's now more than one hundred years old. It's said the stainless-steel façade of the *Admiral* was, in part, inspiration to Eero Saarinen as he was designing the Gateway Arch in 1948. The *Robert E. Lee* is closed and at last visit was moored at a barge just north of the Poplar Street Bridge. A story regarding the *J. S.,* which was so named for its owner John Streckfus, is that when they wintered in New Orleans, Streckfus hired musicians whom he influenced in the creation of a style of music unique to the *J. S.* This music became known as "J.S. music" and with the speech patterns of the Old South the term was slurred to sound like "Jass," which was modified to Jazz. Musician Singleton Palmer, who played the *J. S.,* swore this tale was true, and well it may be.

The Antique Warehouse, a local private museum, has a one-of-a-kind twenty-foot aluminum model of the SS *Admiral* that was built in 1984 to afford the developers a perspective of the boat as they re-created it as a stationary entertainment facility. This model was displayed for some two decades at the local architectural and design offices of HOK. Many of the artifacts housed at the Antique Warehouse, such as the *Admiral,* can be viewed on-line at www.antiquewhs.com. None of the items at this unusual facility are for sale, but the owner, Greg Rhomberg, is always interested in adding to his vast collection of Americana that covers the period from the industrial revolution into the 1960s.

The smallest place, past or present, in this book, is the twenty-eight-foot-square White Castle that for decades anchored the southwest corner of Hampton Avenue and Chippewa Street. Newsboys at that corner peddled the *Globe-Democrat, Star-Times,* and *Post-Dispatch,* and for free reading material there was be the quarterly *White Castle House Organ* placed in a rack just inside the front door. The White Castle publications, which today are true collector's items, extolled the virtues of working for White Castle and depicted the company in glowing terms. These magazines were packed with photos ranging from those of Castle workers to the processing of their prime product, sliders. In those pre-drive-thru days, you avoided a trip into the tiny Castle confines by using the services of their car-hops. Inside, you consumed your burgers from a steel shelf as you stood at the window facing Chippewa or, if you were lucky, you'd get a stool at the counter. A standard menu feature in the 1940s and 1950s were pies that were displayed in a long mirrored case above the "back-bar." The meringue on the chocolate and lemon pies was invariably rubbery in texture, but the Castle hot cocoa was always a frothy delight, as it is today.

The colorful, in more ways than one, Coral Court Motel, with its flat roofs, facades of glazed tile and glass blocks had at its peak seventy-seven units. It was started in 1940 when John Carr bought twenty-nine lots that were part of the Marlborough Manor subdivision. Rather than build a typical motel or tourist court, Carr stayed with the street design concept of Marlborough Manor, thus his complex resembled a small subdivision. The ultra-modern Coral Courts, as it was rightly billed, was somewhat secreted behind a limestone entry with the property well landscaped by shrubbery, trees, and flowers. Over the years, the Coral Court's various neon signs also became landmarks beckoning the throngs of travelers who whisked past on Route 66. And yes, some stopped to get their kicks.

Of the forty-eight locations presented in this volume, all but two are, or were, located within the 1876 boundary of the city of St. Louis. The exceptions are the Parkmoor and Coral Court Motel. The Parkmoor that Marilynne depicts in these pages was at 6737 Clayton Road at Big Bend Boulevard. This location was where they started and ended their sixty-nine-year run. The other St. Louis County Parkmoor was at 10811 Manchester Road at the northwest corner of Lindbergh Boulevard. In St. Louis City, we had a Parkmoor cattycorner from McBride High School at 1728 N. Kingshighway Memorial Boulevard, a block north of KXOK's Radio Park where I premiered my air-name of Johnny Rabbitt some forty-seven years ago and celebrated that first night on AM630 with a Parkmoor Premium Frank with molten cheese along with an order of the best-ever French-fried onion rings and a chocolate malt made with their homemade all-cream ice cream.

Another Parkmoor was at 4206 S. Kingshighway Boulevard at Chippewa Street, and there was one across from Ted Drewes at 6705 Chippewa Street that had replaced an old orange and black frame A&W Root Beer stand. That Parkmoor was designed by noted architect Frank T. Hilliker, one of the founders of Landmarks Association. He also designed the Parkmoor in Indianapolis. The other local Parkmoor was at 324 De Baliviere Avenue between Pershing Avenue and Waterman Boulevard. They also had a location in Springfield, Illinois. The picture in the book brings back many memories of their special Italian spaghetti, the King and the Queen burger, and their wonderful Hot Fudge Angel Food Cake. The Parkmoor always had a contender in the form of Schneithorst's Big Bevo drive-ins first on Hampton Avenue at Wilson Avenue, and then at the site of the current Schneithorst's Kaffee Haus on Lindbergh Boulevard and Clayton Road. Both were under the direction of the Kaffee Haus's current manager Howard Mallott.

Now, it's time to visit some noteworthy St. Louis places and view them in a clear new light that will, I feel, impress, and inspire.

Ron (Johnny Rabbitt) Elz

St. Louis in Watercolor

Riverfront

Although the St. Louis riverfront, in itself, is not architecture, the riverfront is an essential, and often overlooked, aspect of St. Louis's built environment. In addition, the history of the riverfront and the growth of commerce in St. Louis brought thousands of steamboats to the levee with varying degrees of design and detail in their construction. Elegant and simple alike, the steamboat era thrived along St. Louis's riverfront.

Twelve hundred years ago, the ancient people, the Woodland Indians, developed a great urban civilization in the Mississippi and Missouri river valleys and then disappeared four hundred years later. In 1700 the Jesuits established a mission at the mouth of the River des Peres, only to abandon it a few years later. More than fifty years passed before Pierre Laclede selected the present site of St. Louis for a new village in 1764.

Two hundred years ago, the Mississippi River was narrow and swift at St. Louis. The limestone bluff along the riverfront sloped gently to Front Street, ending abruptly in a fifty-foot bank. A flat rock shelf about one hundred feet wide was found at the base of the bluff, which allowed for a low-water towpath. The rear yards of houses facing Main Street extended to the edge of the bluff. St. Louis had already turned its back to the river. A description of the riverfront in 1825 by E. H. Shepard notes that "Front Street, or the levee, was a serrated limestone ledge of rocks."

The wharf was partially improved and paved after 1831 when the last remnants of the stone bluff had disappeared. In 1840 the Mississippi River passed St. Louis in two streams of equal size divided by Bloody Island, the scene of numerous duels.

On August 2, 1817, the steamboat *Zebulon M. Pike* pushed its way up the Mississippi River to dock at St. Louis. The *Zebulon* was the first of thousands of steamboats to ply the waters of St. Louis's riverfront, dock on the cobblestone levee, and transform the town into one of the nation's major cities. By 1850 St. Louis was the second-largest U.S. port, exceeded only by New York. An English visitor in 1858 was impressed by the levee, which "extends along the right bank of the Mississippi for nearly six miles." As many as 170 steamboats had been counted at the St. Louis levee at one time. This was the "Golden Age" of river traffic idealized by Mark Twain and personified by "floating Victorian palaces."

Steamboat traffic grew rapidly with westward expansion. The shallow, flat-bottomed steamboats were essential to pioneering American rivers. The Eagle Packet Company, owned by St. Louisans Henry and William Leyhe, constructed *Young Eagle* in 1861. The packet—a term that refers to a utilitarian steamboat used to transport goods and people—was constructed with materials from salvaged wreckage. The Leyhes remained in the steamboat business for generations, and their final ship, the restaurant *Robert E. Lee*, was constructed in the late 1960s and was a fixture on the riverfront for decades.

Laclede's Landing

Laclede's Landing is named for the city's founder, Pierre Laclede. A vibrant entertainment district, the Landing is the closest a visitor can get to the bustling levee of an age gone by. The narrow cobblestone streets—the nine square blocks directly north of the Eads Bridge—were laid atop the limestone bluffs sloping to the Mississippi River. The Landing is one of the few remnants of the St. Louis levee, of which the majority was demolished to make room for the Arch grounds. Steamboats—filled with cotton from the south, furs from the north and west, and manufactured items from the east—unloaded their goods into the nineteenth-century buildings. The levee was a thriving place of activity and commerce.

In 1849 a fire ignited onboard the steamboat *White Cloud.* Flames spread from ship to ship before jumping to the levee and downtown St. Louis. The damage was extensive, with the majority of downtown needing to being rebuilt. Reconstruction began with a new innovation: cast-iron building fronts. The St. Louis–based Pullis Ironworks prefabricated columns, railings, and sections for cast-iron fronts to replace wooden warehouses. The architecture of Laclede's Landing is typical of pre–Civil War warehouses. The exterior cast iron strengthened the building and protected the valuable contents within, while the interior was utilitarian and vast.

St. Louis was once the booming center of the colonial fur trade, and echoes of trappers' footsteps are mixed with today's music from the nightclubs along the cobblestone streets. Clamorgan Alley was named in honor of Jacques Clamorgan, who arrived in St. Louis in 1780. He was a fur trader, slave trader, merchant, financier, and land speculator, and he owned much of the levee. His Missouri Company preceded Lewis and Clark in sending expeditions up the Missouri River to find an overland route to the Pacific. His home was located at the current site of the Christian Peper Tobacco Building (Raeder Place) on First Street. The chain restaurant the Old Spaghetti Factory occupies the lower level of the building today. The Missouri Hotel also occupied this site in 1820. Missouri's first state constitution was drafted and adopted in this hotel.

Clamorgan's four mulatto children received an estate of nearly one thousand dollars. One of his sons, Cyprian Clamorgan, was a member of a small group that Cyprian described in his 1858 publication *The Colored Aristocracy of St. Louis.* Part of Jacques Clamorgan's estate was placed in the name of his slave, Esther. This Spanish land grant in St. Louis is one of the earliest on record. She was freed and claimed the land but lost the settlement. Her land is where the Schoelhorn-Albrecht Machine Company building now stands; a plaque on the building designates her ownership.

The indestructible pre–Civil War warehouses sat for nearly one hundred years and endured silent neglect. Much of this area was ripe for demolition when the Jefferson National Expansion site cleared the land along the levee, but the destruction of buildings halted at the Eads Bridge, the south boundary of the Landing. Other than some industrial and abandoned buildings south of the Arch grounds, the Landing is the last surviving, and thriving, link to the city when it not only faced but was also dependent on the river for success and survival.

In 1975 the Laclede's Landing Redevelopment Corporation was formed, a revitalization plan was adopted, and renovation of the buildings began. Offices, shops, restaurants, galleries, casinos, and nightclubs moved into the vast area of warehouses and vacant lots.

Losses continue, however. The vacant building of the Bronson Hide Company, built in 1856, deteriorated and was demolished in 1997. Plans for redevelopment of the Switzer Candy Company, built in 1874, vanished when a disastrous storm hit the structure in 2006. Faded lettering—advertising of bygone businesses—remains in view on weather-worn brick walls.

Old Rock House

The Old Rock House was the oldest standing building in St. Louis when President Franklin D. Roosevelt proclaimed the Jefferson National Expansion Memorial in 1935. Manuel Lisa quarried the limestone from his property on the river bluffs and built a fur-trading warehouse of stone in 1818. The Rock House was located on Chestnut and First streets, the current site of the north stairway leading to the Jefferson National Expansion Museum.

In 1828 James Clemens, Jr.—a cousin of Mark Twain—purchased the warehouse. Clemens must have shared some of his cousin's luck, since the Old Rock House, the Old Courthouse, and the Old Cathedral were among the few notable survivors of the Great Fire of 1849. From 1849 to 1865, John Clemens (another relative of Mark Twain) manufactured sails and canvas for covered wagons in the building. Dred Scott worked at this company during his freedom trial at the Old Courthouse.

During the 1890s the famous musician W. C. Handy frequently performed in the Old Rock House Saloon. When purchased by the National Park Service in 1936, the building housed the saloon on the first floor, a nightclub on second floor, and small bedrooms on the third. Built into the natural bluff overlooking the river, the original building had only three sides, the fourth (west) side being composed of the limestone bluff itself.

Between 1939 and 1942, forty square blocks of the riverfront were demolished to make room for the Jefferson National Expansion Memorial. The Old Rock House was a part of this demolition. In 1943 the Works Progress Administration (WPA) rebuilt the historic structure. However, just sixteen years after it was restored, the Old Rock House was dismantled to make way for a railroad tunnel essential to the construction of the Gateway Arch.

The structure was carefully dismantled for an eventual reconstruction, but due to the continued demolition and reconstruction, very few original limestone blocks existed. The remaining original building material was reassembled as an exhibit in the Old Courthouse.

Old Courthouse

The Old Courthouse was constructed on land donated by Judge John Lucas and René Auguste Chouteau. For years the location served as a center of civil and legal activities, and today it is a part of the Jefferson National Expansion Memorial.

In 1828 construction was completed on a Federal-style courthouse. St. Louis quickly outgrew this small brick building, and in 1839 architect Henry Singleton laid the groundwork for a Greek Revival structure, using the existing courthouse as the east wing of the new construction. Singleton used a plan derived from Andrea Palladio's Renaissance design of the Villa Rotunda, built in 1567–70 in Italy, a square covered by a dome with four wings jutting from the center. Construction neared completion in the mid-1840s, in time to welcome the first national railroad convention into the rotunda. Senator Thomas H. Benton spoke to the delegates, advocating a transcontinental railroad.

The structure was one of the few not destroyed in the Great Fire of 1849. Two years later, architect Robert Mitchell began major renovations, which were highlighted by the demolition and reconstruction of the east wing—the original city courthouse. The west wing also had major renovations in the 1850s. Mitchell built large office wings where the north and south porticos had been planned. For a time, the north wing served as City Hall.

From 1860 to 1864, architect William Rumbold replaced the wooden cupola with an Italian Renaissance dome modeled after St. Paul's Cathedral in London. An engineering marvel, this 128-ton, cast-iron dome was the first of its kind in the United States, with the Capitol in Washington, D.C., still under construction. It was the first building to utilize cast iron as a frame for a dome. All future capitol domes found their inspiration from this design.

Towering 192 feet high, the Courthouse was the tallest building in nineteenth-century St. Louis. It dominated the city's skyline. Steamboat captains could take their bearings from the flagpole atop the dome.

Inside the dome, Carl Wimar painted the first murals west of the Mississippi in 1862. The paintings have been restored several times. The east wing contains one of the building's unique features: An iron staircase spirals thirty-two feet from the basement to the third floor with no vertical braces and without support from beneath.

Many important trials, speeches, debates, and rallies occurred in the Courthouse, most notably the Dred Scott case, which changed the course of the nation. In 1859 Ulysses S. Grant freed his only slave on the Courthouse steps. Suffragist Virginia Louisa Minor sued for women's right to vote in 1872. Joseph Pulitzer bought the bankrupt *Dispatch* newspaper at public auction on the east steps in 1878.

In 1940 the Old Courthouse was deeded to the federal government by the city of St. Louis. Two of the historic courtrooms are restored. The dome has been renovated. Galleries exhibit paintings and photographs that relate to the history of westward expansion.

A bronze plaque pays tribute to the nearby site of Fort San Carlos, and a granite boulder commemorates the beginning of the first trail west: the Daniel Boone trail.

Lafayette Park

Lafayette Park was established in 1836 as the first public park in St. Louis and the oldest park west of the Mississippi. The land began as thirty acres of common fields, a communal area for agricultural development and livestock grazing. As plots of the common fields were being sold off to private owners for homes, Mayor John Darby and Board of Aldermen President Colonel Thornton Grimsley introduced the ordinance to create the park. Colonel Grimsley first used the park for weekly cavalry maneuvers with his Home Guard unit, the "Grays." The drilling led early residents to call the land the "parade ground" or "Grimsley's Folly."

After nearly two turbulent decades, the land surrounding the park was dedicated as Lafayette Square in 1851, and home construction began in earnest. Four Italianate estates were built on the southern side of the park by prominent civic leaders, including Charles Gibson, who championed the neighborhood for the next fifty years.

Speculators bought land on the north side. Montgomery Blair purchased some of the north property in 1857. Blair was appointed postmaster general of the United States by President Lincoln and moved to Washington, D.C. He sold his plot at 2043 Park Avenue to William Huse. Architect George I. Barnett designed a mansion worthy of Huse's wealth. The plans were the same dimensions and style as Barnett's design for the executive mansion in Jefferson City. Barnett, a prominent St. Louis architect in mid-nineteenth-century St. Louis, built a number of significant structures in St. Louis in addition to homes in Lafayette Square, including the North Grand Water Tower and Henry Shaw's country house in the Missouri Botanical Garden.

After the Civil War, improvements were made to the park. Wealthy residents in the surrounding homes purchased bonds to hire Maximilian Kern, one of the first landscape architects in the United States. Manicured gardens and thousands of tree varieties were planted with a five-foot, three-inch wrought-iron fence enclosing the park. Harriet Hosmer's Thomas Hart Benton statue was placed on a knoll. A bronze cast of Houdon's statue of George Washington soon followed. Cannons from a British warship from the Revolutionary War were scattered throughout the park.

Active social gatherings took place. Cricket matches replaced the drilling militia. A grotto and a central lake were developed. Weekly concerts were held in a bandstand pavilion constructed in 1872. The horses pulling carriages around the park drank at the extravagant watering trough at the entrance to Benton Place. In the 1870s Lafayette Square was the most fashionable place to live in St. Louis City. Extravagant Victorian mansions with mansard roofs and wrought-iron detail surrounded the park.

On the night of May 27, 1896, at 5 p.m., disaster struck. A tornado hit Lafayette Square with full force. The statues of Benton and Washington were all that remained. Many of the magnificent trees were reduced to kindling. Mansions lost their roofs, and walls became piles of rubble. Decay set in. Because of a depression and the First World War, the wealthy couldn't afford to rebuild, and their mansions were converted into rooming houses.

The renaissance of the 1970s and low prices brought back urban pioneers to renovate the mansions and return them to their past glory. Today the park and square are reliving their new cosmopolitan lifestyle.

Christ Church Cathedral

The first Episcopal congregation west of the Mississippi River was organized in 1819. Their first church, a modest structure, opened in 1829 at the corner of Third and Chestnut streets. The present English Gothic Christ Church Cathedral was designed by Leopold Eidlitz and constructed at Thirteenth and Locust streets amidst the turbulence of the Civil War. The cornerstone was laid April 22, 1860.

On Christmas Day 1867, the doors opened for the first worship service. The urban setting for the cathedral seemed fitting and recalled how most European Gothic churches served as a gathering place in the center of town.

The walls are of sandstone, which was quarried in East St. Louis and ferried across the Mississippi. This building with its added limestone tower ranks among America's first examples of the fourteenth-century English Gothic. The exterior is simple in design, with tall narrow windows and a steeply pitched roof.

The Mary E. Bofinger Chapel, funded by a wealthy steamboat operator in memory of his wife, was added in 1894. The chapel floor is a columbarium, the church's only burial place. Each engraved floor tile covers a vault containing the cremated remains of the person named. The tower and entrance were added from 1910 to 1912.

The elegant rib vaults supporting the roof fan out into lace-like designs. The awe-inspiring reredos—an ornamental screen adorned with sculpture and tracery—rises behind the high altar of the church. It comprises fifty-two completely carved religious figures, leading to the central figure of a crucified Christ. It is modeled after the high altar screen at Winchester Cathedral in England. Harry Hems sculpted each piece from a cream-colored stone mined in England, then they were shipped to St. Louis. To commemorate the similarity of the Cathedral's reredos to the altar screens in St. Albans Abbey Cathedral and Winchester Cathedral in England, stones from each English church have been set into the structure of the building. The Tiffany windows were a gift to the church in 1917, and a new organ was installed in 1965.

The Cathedral has conducted classical and sacred music concerts for nearly 150 years. The Shepley Program of Music and Art continues that tradition and hosts free concerts featuring local, national, and international talents.

Water Towers

In the United States, there are reputedly only seven surviving historic standpipe towers—water towers used to relieve water pressure surges—and St. Louis is home to three of them. True water towers are generally shorter and more massive, as opposed to the tall, thin profiles of standpipe towers. These towers are purely decorative, concealing the five-foot-wide, one-hundred-foot-high metal standpipes that helped smoothly circulate water into surrounding homes. St. Louis's water towers are well preserved and have been declared historic landmarks.

The East Grand Water Tower, a 154-foot stuccoed white brick Corinthian column, is the largest perfect Corinthian column in the world. George Barnett designed it in 1871 during U. S. Grant's presidency. It served as an aviation beacon in the 1920s. The lights were extinguished during World War II as a security precaution but were reactivated in 1949 to guide flyers to Lambert Field.

Just a few blocks over, the Bissell Water Tower, a 196-foot red brick tower, was erected in 1886 at Bissell and Blair streets. William Eames designed the tower to resemble a Muslim minaret. Its height reached 206 feet when new high service pumps were installed in the waterworks at Bissell Point. A spiral staircase leads to a lookout platform at the top. There was an attempt in 1958 to raze the tower, but a group of concerned citizens halted the plan.

Southwest of downtown, the Compton Hill Water Tower was built on one of the highest locations in the city in the thirty-six-acre Compton Hill Reservoir Park. The reservoir, in the center of a landscaped park, was constructed in 1867 to supply clarified water to the city. The 179-foot tower was completed in 1898. Using in a medieval Romanesque design, architect Harvey Ellis—who also worked on City Hall—detailed heavy, rusticated limestone with a carved griffin and vine-like scrolls. Atop the 198 steps that spiral around the standpipe, an observation platform offers a 360-degree panoramic scene of St. Louis. During the 1904 World's Fair, many visitors enjoyed touring this St. Louis landmark. The lighted brick and limestone tower soars above Grand Avenue, serving as a beacon to today's travelers on Interstate 44.

Old Post Office

More than 123 years after General William Tecumseh Sherman's 1884 dedication of the Old Post Office and Custom House, the 242,000-square-foot historic landmark is still breathing new life into downtown St. Louis. In Sherman's day, the building symbolized the city's emergence as the hub of the post–Civil War expansion westward. Today, it symbolizes the city's rejuvenation.

Architect Alfred Bult Mullett, supervising architect of the U.S. Treasury, was influenced in his design by the construction of the Louvre in Paris. Like the Louvre, the building combines an Italian Renaissance palace with the addition of a mansard roof. It is an excellent example of Second Empire–style architecture. The three floors mirror the Greek orders of architecture: Doric, Ionic, and Corinthian columns as used in the Roman Coliseum. The exterior spared no expense. Most notably, *Miss America of War and Miss America of Peace,* an early sculpture by Daniel Chester French, who later designed the colossal seated figure of Lincoln in Washington, D.C., crowns the Eighth Street pediment formed against the dome.

The Old Post Office and Custom House occupies an entire city block in downtown St. Louis. The French-influenced building was constructed between 1872 and 1884. Because a quicksand bog was discovered on the construction site, four feet of concrete were poured over log pilings with cotton bales packed between them to provide a stable base. The most advanced construction technologies were applied to the building, primarily with the use of cast-iron columns and wrought-iron I beams.

The Old Post Office was designed as a fortress with a thirty-foot-deep moat and sliding iron shutters with rifle ports on the windows. One of only three U.S. subtreasuries was located on the premises. The subtreasury, in addition to the fresh memories of the Civil War, made safeguards necessary. The site of the building was also key, located between the Eads Bridge and the Union Depot, which were connected by a tunnel. The tunnel allowed trains to be loaded on-site, but smoke from the trains proved overwhelming for the building's circulation, and the tunnel access was blocked off.

The building was used as the Eight Circuit Court of Appeals from 1884 to 1933, with many famous cases handled in the courtrooms. The court upheld the breakup of Standard Oil in 1909, and they ruled on the Teapot Dome scandal of the Harding administration. Today, part of the building is used as a downtown campus for Webster University. The Missouri Court of Appeals, Eastern District, moved in, joining other state offices and businesses in the newly renovated landmark.

Little Bohemia

At the corner of Fourth and Clark streets, this downtown saloon and art gallery served as an after-hours center for artists to debate and interpret the aesthetic truths of the latest bohemian topics. Members of the Washington University School of Fine Arts faculty occupied the corner table by the window and discussed their latest endeavors while mocking the upper classes. The brick walls were covered with their most recent works of art portraying the state of world politics.

Jay Landesman, one of the saloon's owner, focused his attention on running a family antique business, but he was also a proficient writer, artist, and entrepreneur. He was the founder of the Crystal Palace cabaret, a famous venue and cornerstone of Gaslight Square, which hosted entertainers such as the Kingston Trio, Barbra Streisand, and the Smothers Brothers. In 1948, while operating Little Bohemia, Landesman founded *Neurotica,* a poetry magazine "by and for neurotics," the bible for St. Louis's Beat Generation. Little Bohemia served as a distribution point for the first issue.

Architecturally, this block of stores was of distinctive Creole design. In this style, the walls were frequently built of French-style bricks between posts, and the roof slanted front to back or may have been hipped at one or both ends. Decorative jigsaw embellishments were added to the second-floor galleries and living quarters. Scrolling brackets of hand-wrought iron from the forge—just two or three feet deep—supported the second-floor balcony. The cast-iron "gallery" of later vintage was different—wide and supported on columns, all cast from molds in commercial foundries. The wrought-iron filigree added the charm reminiscent of New Orleans's French Quarter.

Across the street the Tums headquarters still stands, ready to save the night of too many draughts. The bar and other buildings on the block were torn down for the Regal Riverfront Hotel—now the Millennium Hotel—known for its revolving skyline restaurant.

Union Station

St. Louis Union Station was once the largest and busiest railroad terminal in the world. Designed by Theodore C. Link in 1896 at a cost of $6.5 million, the majestic station is a mix of Richardsonian and French Romanesque styles.

Link found inspiration in both antiquity and the Middle Ages. He looked toward the Basilica of Constantine—the largest structure of the Roman Forum—for the sixty-five-foot barrel-vaulted ceiling that spans the Grand Hall. Likewise, he was inspired by the medieval fortified French town of Carcassone for the imposing clock tower that has become such a mainstay on St. Louis's skyline.

Link's architectural plan is most impressive when entering the station's Grand Hall, with its sweeping archways, fresco and gold leaf detailing, mosaics, and art glass windows. A "whispering arch" over the stair entrance dominates the main waiting room. A person on one side of the arch can hear whispers murmured on the other side.

The allegorical window is another highlight of the ornate interior of the Grand Hall. This hand-made stained-glass window is stationed above the main entryway and is representative of three legs of the transcontinental railroad: New York, St. Louis, and San Francisco. The window was designed by St. Louis artist Sylvester Annan.

The Train Shed lies to the south of the Headhouse, and the shed's eleven-plus acres made it the largest in the world. Designed by George H. Pegram, the shed contained thirty-two tracks and gates consisting of nearly nineteen miles of track. The steel truss structure was covered by a series of arches.

The station closed to traffic in 1978, and the building fell into disrepair. Seven years and $150 million later, the St. Louis Union Station was renovated into a hotel and shopping and restaurant district. The Grand Hall is now the Hyatt Regency's lobby, and the Train Shed consists of nightclubs, restaurants, and shops.

Aloe Plaza

In 1901 the city of St. Louis planned to demolish a rundown area of buildings across the street from Union Station to create a central parkway along Market Street. Louis P. Aloe, who served as president of the Board of Aldermen from 1916 to 1923, spearheaded the passage of a major bond issue. The $87 million bond issue passed in Aloe's last year in office. The bond issue included money to widen Market Street and construct Aloe Plaza across from Union Station.

In 1936 the city commissioned a fountain for the plaza from renowned Swedish sculptor Carl Milles, an acquaintance of Aloe's widow, Edith, and an apprentice of the famous French sculptor Auguste Rodin. The cast-bronze fountain was dedicated on May 11, 1940, after remaining hidden from public view for months.

The Wedding of the Rivers, as it was originally named, represents the confluence of the Mississippi and Missouri rivers. The union of rivers is depicted by two central nude figures, the Mississippi as a male and the Missouri as a female. Symbolized in Greek mythology as water sprites, mermaids, and fish, seventeen smaller streams join the two main rivers. A puritanical uproar arose over the nudity of the central figures. In response, the city changed the name of the fountain to *The Meeting of the Waters.* No changes were made to the fountain group itself.

After the unveiling of the Milles fountain the editorial page in the *St. Louis Post-Dispatch* applauded the design. The newspaper said of the sculpted figures: "Are they grotesque? Are they unclothed? The questions are as extraneous as they would be in watching a school of porpoises or a flock of lambs at play."

City Hall

In 1840 the city of St. Louis bought a six-acre plot of land, which included part the Chouteau's Pond tract. For nearly half a century the land served as Washington Square Park. During these decades, city government was run from a number of places, including the Old Courthouse and, starting in 1872, an inadequate building on Eleventh Street. By the late 1800s, Washington Square Park was considered a primary location for a new city hall.

The city hall construction was budgeted at $2 million. An 1890 architectural competition was won by architect George Mann of the St. Joseph–based firm of Eckel & Mann. The winning design was a French-style plan inspired by the Hotel de Ville, or City Hall, of Paris. The impressive dormer windows—or belvederes—were inspired by the Chateau de Chambord on the Loire River. Pierre Laclede's aristocratic origins were recalled in this pretentious building for the city.

On July 19, 1890, Mayor Edward Noonan's daughter dug the first shovelful of dirt to begin the construction. A year later, on June 6, 1891, the cornerstone was laid. Workers took fourteen years to complete the structure, in time for the 1904 World's Fair. The total cost to build it was $1,787,159, well under budget.

This sumptuous four-story building is 380 feet by 205 feet and faces Tucker Boulevard. The building is constructed of granite, brick, sandstone, and limestone. The first floor is Missouri pink granite, with the remaining floors constructed of pink-orange Roman brick. For many years the building's composition appeared to be dark limestone, due to its coal-blackened exterior covering the original brightness. A thorough cleaning revealed its true colors. The French Renaissance roof is a burgundy-red glazed Spanish tile.

The exterior of City Hall was never finished. Decorations were meant to be carved on limestone around the sides of the dormers. Three towers that were built were removed in 1936: an eighty-foot bell tower that rose above the main entrance on Tucker Boulevard, and nineteen-foot towers flanking it. Major structural flaws and corrosion were discovered when the building's roof was being replaced.

The interior of City Hall is as lavish as the exterior, highlighted by the four-story, white Italian marble lobby located just inside the Tucker Boulevard entrance. The skylighted ceiling of the lobby is framed with gold glass and rests above a gold-finished plaster molding. The grand staircase is opposite the main entrance and branches into two directions halfway to the second floor. Balustraded balconies on each of the upper three stories overlook the ground floor.

The words "City Hall" were carved above the doors on the street entrances to counteract Mayor Bernard Dickmann's plan to place neon signs above the doors in red, white, and blue.

Brookings Hall

Washington University began building its Hilltop Campus—now the Danforth Campus—in 1899. The tree-lined driveways to the broad steps leading to the arch of Brookings Hall are a superb approach to the Gothic campus. It didn't take long for construction on the new home of Washington University to start. Robert S. Brookings was responsible for moving Washington University to its current, permanent location, and he contributed $200,000 to the university for the construction of an administrative building, later named in his honor. Distinguished by its Collegiate Gothic architecture, Brookings Hall is inspired by St. John's College in Cambridge.

The inscription on the east facade of the hall reads, *Discere Si Cupias Intra: Salvere Iubemus,* meaning, "If you wish to learn, enter: we welcome you." The inscription above the clock on the west facade reads, *Cedunt Horae, Opera Manent:* "The hours go by, the works remain."

By 1901 several buildings on the Hilltop Campus were completed, funded by donations from civic leaders who, in addition to Brookings, included Adolphus Busch, Samuel Cupples, Elizabeth Liggett, and Stephen Ridgley. Brookings Quadrangle is made up of four of the first campus buildings, named for their donors: Brookings, Busch, Cupples, and Ridgley Halls.

At the turn of the century, however, the university was experiencing tough financial times. Fortunately, its high vantage point on the hilltop allowed an excellent view of one of the most ambitious endeavors that St. Louis ever embarked on: the Louisiana Purchase Exposition. Brookings, president of Washington University's Board of Trustees, leased the campus to David R. Francis and the Louisiana Purchase Exposition Company. This agreement solved the university's financial issues and offered the Exposition Company more space—a commodity that was in short supply.

The Brookings Quadrangle buildings played significant roles during the Fair. Francis used Brookings Hall as his chief administration building. Architects and engineers took up residence in Busch Hall, while Cupples Hall hosted ethnological exhibits. Ridgley Hall hosted the international congresses—gatherings of scholars and intellectuals from around the world. Finally, Francis Field and Gymnasium, a new addition to the campus, hosted the 1904 Olympic Games.

Francis Field and Gymnasium

Washington University's Francis Field and Gymnasium hosted the 1904 Olympic Games, the third modern Olympiad and the first international games held in the western hemisphere. The gymnasium and the athletic field are named in honor of David R. Francis, president of the Louisiana Purchase Exposition. Francis—former mayor of St. Louis, governor of Missouri, ambassador to Russia during its revolution, and alumnus of Washington University—was responsible for bringing the Olympic Games to the Hilltop Campus. Officially known as the Games of the III Olympiad, they were held from May 14 to November 23, 1904, although the "official" track and field games were held in a six-day period in late August and early September. Amateur athletic associations sponsored the majority of U.S. contenders, and only six other countries entered athletes. The United States won twenty-one of the twenty-two track and field events.

In tune with the campus, Francis Gymnasium's architecture is Collegiate Gothic and constructed of Indiana limestone and Missouri red granite. The gym has since become the centerpiece of a major athletic complex.

Francis Field, built in 1902, has received nearly a complete facelift. The wrought-iron entry gate—erected in 1914—serves as a memorial to the Olympics. The first stands were constructed of

reinforced concrete, one of the first fields to use this technology. Following the Olympics, the field became the permanent home of the school's football team, the Bears. In the early 1980s, the third-of-a-mile (660-yard) track was replaced with a synthetic 400-meter track. The stands, which held 19,000 fans, were replaced with 4,000-seat stands, along with concessions, a press box, and other amenities.

On October 11, 1992, the athletic complex hosted the first nationally televised three-candidate debate, among Bill Clinton, George H. W. Bush, and Ross Perot. Washington University laid out the red carpet for the candidates, right over the hardwood floor of the gymnasium.

In July 1994, Francis Field was a centerpiece for the U.S. Olympic Festival. Three thousand athletes lived on the 169-acre Hilltop Campus.

Ridgley Hall

Ridgley Hall was Washington University's first library on the Hilltop Campus and was named for Stephen Ridgley, a British-born businessman and statesman who was elected to the Missouri State Senate in 1866. Ridgley provided $76,000 for the fire-proof library. Ridgley died in 1892, more than a decade before Ridgley Hall was completed.

Like the rest of the campus, the structure is built of Missouri pink granite and trimmed with Bedford limestone. Cope & Stewardson, a Philadelphia-based architectural firm, designed Ridgley Hall and the others on the quadrangle. The firm found inspiration in the architecture of Cambridge and Oxford universities. The style of architecture is Collegiate Gothic, which gained its name from the popularity of Gothic architecture that swept college campuses in the late nineteenth and early twentieth centuries. Prominent examples of Collegiate Gothic architecture include Princeton University, University of Pennsylvania, Yale University, and Boston College.

Ridgley's arcade was inspired by Canterbury Quadrangle at St. John's College at Oxford. The university library moved into Ridgley Hall in January 1905, after the World's Fair. Ridgley Library was one of the campus showpieces. The library has a monumental reading room with high windows and an ornate plaster ceiling, and the closed stacks were built for 40,000 volumes. The reading room is now called Holmes Lounge.

Forest Park

At 1,296 acres, Forest Park is one of the largest urban parks in the country, surpassing New York's Central Park by nearly 500 acres. The land was purchased in 1875 for $799,995. When dedicated in 1876, the park was a dense forest four miles from downtown St. Louis. Maximilian Kern was given the commission to tame it into a carriage park similar to Central Park. He had previously designed Lafayette Park as a strolling park in 1864.

Forest Park was selected over Carondelet Park, O'Fallon Park, and other locations as the site of the 1904 World's Fair, and the park's landscape would forever be altered. On October 1, 1901, the Louisiana Purchase Exposition took control of 657 acres—the western half of the park. Much of the forest that gave the park its name was quickly leveled to make room for the temporary extravagance of the Fair under the guidance of landscape architect George Kessler.

Although the vast majority of the World's Fair attractions were built of staff—an impermanent and inexpensive mixture of plaster of Paris and hemp—some structures were built to last. The Palace of Fine Arts—today's Saint Louis Art Museum—is the only original palace remaining, although the Bird Cage at the Saint Louis Zoo and the Grand Basin remain. After the Fair, the Jefferson Memorial—today's Missouri History Museum—was constructed at the main entrance to the Fair, and the World's Fair Pavilion was built where the burned Missouri State Building stood.

Forest Park is a natural oasis in an urban environment for residents and tourists who visit the park each year. A number of nonprofit organizations work with St. Louis City to maintain and improve the amenities of the park. Forest Park Forever was founded in 1986, and the Flora Conservancy was founded in 1999.

The city of St. Louis and Forest Park Forever embarked on the Forest Park Master Plan in 1995. The Master Plan was developed in response to deterioration of the park's built landscape. The nearly $100 million endeavor not only improved the infrastructure of, maintenance of, and access to the park, but also enhanced visitor experiences with new amenities.

Art Museum

The Palace of Fine Arts was the only World's Fair palace constructed to remain permanently in Forest Park. Due to the nature of its holdings, the building needed to be fireproof. Instead of using staff—a mixture of plaster of Paris and hemp—renowned architect Cass Gilbert constructed the Palace of Fine Arts out of Bedford limestone and Roman brick at a cost of $1 million, twice the cost of the other palaces.

In addition, Gilbert's design was remarkably simple when compared to other palaces. Gilbert used the Roman-influenced Neoclassical style with Corinthian colonnades to design the exterior. He was inspired by the soaring arches of the Roman Baths of Caracalla. The side buildings were removed after the Fair, leaving the central hall and its galleries for the new home of the Saint Louis Art Museum. The museum, founded in 1879 as Washington University's Saint Louis School and Museum of Fine Arts, relocated to its new, permanent home from downtown St. Louis. The museum separated from the university in 1909.

With its seventy-eight-foot-high vaulted ceiling and sixty-foot span, the Sculpture Hall is a prime example of Roman architecture. Galleries branch off from the main hall. Period rooms, decorative arts, and primitive, native, and Indian art fill the galleries on the lower level. Twentieth-century works and current styles are displayed on the second floor. The permanent collections are supplemented regularly by special exhibitions, which bring art treasures from all over the world to St. Louis.

The museum had two major renovations—in the 1950s and 1970s—which added, among other elements, an auditorium and a restaurant. A third major renovation is scheduled.

The Saint Louis Art Museum is fronted by a prominent symbol of the city: The *Apotheosis of St. Louis.* The sculpture, which now overlooks Art Hill and the Grand Basin, was created by Charles Niehaus and welcomed visitors at the grand entrance to the World's Fair, near the Missouri History Museum.

Two other World's Fair statues of note grace the exterior of the Art Museum: Daniel Chester French's *Sculpture* and Louis St. Gaudens's *Painting.* Both statues were originally made of staff for the Fair, but the artists were later commissioned to carve their works in limestone for permanent display. Also, above the portico and Corinthian columns are six statues representing six great periods of art: Classical, Oriental, Egyptian, Renaissance, Gothic, and Modern.

Grand Basin

In 1901, city planner and landscape architect George Kessler was a major player in transforming forests, thickets, swamps, and farmland into the glory and elegance of the 1904 World's Fair. After the Fair, he was charged with the task of shaping the parkland into the creative idealism, order, and urban spatial discipline of a tamed Forest Park.

The Grand Basin was the geographic focal point of the World's Fair, and it was the center of a large and complex water system. The Cascades, a series of terraced waterfalls that poured down Art Hill, fed the basin. From the Grand Basin, an interconnected series of lagoons, canals, fountains, and water effects wound through the fairgrounds.

Kessler and Emmanuel Masqueray, chief designer of the World's Fair exhibition, coordinated the creation of the waterways, which contained more than 25 million gallons of water. Leading up to the Fair, improving water problems was a primary concern for the city of St. Louis. The city's water supply was improved. The River des Peres, which snaked through the western half of Forest Park, was carefully, and permanently, rerouted to an underground channel. More than 2,870 feet of four-by-four-foot brick ductwork were laid as a mainline drainage system for the fairgrounds, and hydraulic pumps were installed to keep water in circulation.

After the Fair, the Grand Basin was sized down but remained a central element of the park. Time, neglect, and deterioration ruined the use and aesthetic presence of the basin. As the centerpiece of the Forest Park Master Plan, in 2004 the Grand Basin received a $4 million renovation. The basin was drained, the walls were replaced, water fountains were added, waterways to lagoons were reconnected, and boat landings were added. New bridges passing over streams lead into and out of the basin. Stairways lead down to the water, where geysers spray rowboats carrying visitors.

Today's Grand Basin—with its fountains, bridges, and view of the Art Museum—has again become a centerpiece attraction for visitors to Forest Park, and much of the grandeur from the World's Fair has been restored.

Bird Cage

The Smithsonian Institution's contribution to the 1904 World's Fair was a Flight Cage of curved structural steel beams placed eight feet apart and covered with steel mesh. Frank Baker, superintendent of the National Zoo, a part of the Smithsonian Institution, designed the structure. This walk-through aviary was the largest free-flight birdcage in the world, at 228 feet long, 84 feet wide, and 50 feet high, and it was divided lengthwise into two sections. The structure cost $17,500 to construct.

After the Fair, the Smithsonian was ready to dismantle the aviary, return it to the National Zoo in Washington, D.C., and reconstruct it in their zoological gardens. On December 11, 1904, just ten days after the Fair had closed, the *St. Louis Post-Dispatch* reported: "There is some danger that the big bird cage at the World's Fair may be pulled in two in the tug-of-war for its possession which is being waged, with the city of St. Louis holding to one end and the Smithsonian Institution of Washington pulling at the other end." After finding out that other organizations were interested in purchasing it, the city of St. Louis bought it in 1905, without the birds, for $3,500.

The purchase of the Flight Cage inspired citizens of St. Louis to vote to construct the first municipally supported zoo in the nation. In north St. Louis a previous zoo had its beginnings in 1876 in Fairgrounds Park. It consisted of a bear pit and a primate house. In 1916 these two attractions were moved to seventy-seven acres set aside near the cage in Forest Park to help establish the Saint Louis Zoo.

The Flight Cage is now called the 1904 World's Fair Flight Cage and Edward K. Love Conservation Foundation Cypress Swamp. In 2003–04, the cage underwent a massive renovation and was transformed into a cypress swamp. It reopened in 2005 to exhibit native Missouri animals and ecosystems in a Mississippi river habitat.

World's Fair Pavilion

The World's Fair Pavilion was not constructed as part of the 1904 World's Fair. Instead, it was built as a memorial from the proceeds of the Fair.

The Louisiana Purchase Exposition Company had pledged to restore Forest Park back to its intended use, and one of the company's first gifts to the city was the pavilion. In 1909 the company hired architect Henry Wright to design an open-air structure to be constructed atop Government Hill. The site commands a dramatic view of Forest Park, and during the Fair, it was the location of the Missouri Building, which was destroyed by fire.

Wright designed the World's Fair Pavilion in a Spanish adobe style of architecture with stucco walls and a red tiled roof, a popular trend of the day. The pavilion cost $35,000 to build. Sitting at the highest point of the park, the pavilion receives cool breezes, creating a respite during St. Louis' hot summers. The wide archways provide an exposed area for entertaining, picnics, receptions, and special events.

Landscape architect George Kessler was charged with returning the fairgrounds to an urban park. For Government Hill, Kessler designed a terraced hill with a central fountain and grand staircases leading up to the pavilion. The design is an excellent example of Beaux Arts formalism. Unlike similar contemporary designs, Kessler's work proved both aesthetic and functional.

Time and neglect deteriorated the building. The original brick under the stucco exterior had disintegrated due to years of weather damage. Age and the lack of maintenance had caused the fountain and pathways to erode. In 1998, as part of the Forest Park Master Plan, Forest Park Forever and the city of St. Louis raised $1.1 million to totally renovate the building. Boarded up walls were taken down to reveal the salon-like space. A history wall has been added to recount the building's past. Today, the pavilion remains a popular location for special events.

Jefferson Memorial

At Lindell and DeBaliviere, the Jefferson Memorial Building stands at the former grand entrance to the 1904 World's Fair. The memorial was built in 1913 at a cost of $450,000 with proceeds from the 1904 World's Fair. The two-story white limestone structure is Classical Revival and designed by Isaac Taylor and Oscar Enders. The original building consisted of two wings separated by an open portico with a forty-five-ton marble statue of Thomas Jefferson greeting visitors. Karl Bitter, director of sculpture of the 1904 World's Fair, arranged to have a block of marble shipped to the site, where he carved the statue on its pedestal. A bronze relief sculpture, also cast by Bitter, called *Signing the Louisiana Treaty* is attached to an interior wall.

The building is now known as the Missouri History Museum (MHM), formerly called the Missouri Historical Society, which took posession of the east wing of the building soon after construction was completed. The west wing was used as a civic meeting space for a number of years until MHM took control of the entire building, officially in 1947.

MHM was founded in 1866 and collects and preserves the history of St. Louis, the state of Missouri, and the American West. The collections at MHM have national significance. In addition to the vast 1904 World's Fair collection, MHM holds many personal artifacts from explorer William Clark and aviator Charles Lindbergh. The costume collection is the sixth largest of its kind in the nation. The Creole furniture at MHM is the largest collection of Missouri-made Creole furniture in existence. Also, the library and archives—located at a separate location where artifacts not on display are stored—has a vast collection of material on the American West.

The Jefferson Memorial Building received a series of renovations in the late twentieth and early twenty-first centuries. In the early 1980s, MHM expanded southward with a glass-enclosed basement loggia. In 2000, the Emerson Center was completed, replacing the additions from the 1980s. The St. Louis–based architectural firm Hellmuth, Obata & Kassabaum used an environmental design to maximize energy usage while protecting the artifacts. The 92,000-square-foot, glass-enclosed Emerson Center tripled the size of the museum and includes four galleries, a 347-seat auditorium, three classrooms, a resource center, a restaurant, a gift shop, and space to host major traveling exhibitions.

Nathan Frank Bandstand

The original Forest Park bandstand was a wooden music pagoda built about the time the park was dedicated in 1876. Concerts were held there before and after renovation for the 1904 World's Fair. John Philip Sousa performed often at the pagoda. The bandstand gradually fell into disrepair, and a storm hurried its demise in the late 1910s.

In July 1924, St. Louis lawyer Nathan Frank donated funds to reconstruct the pagoda as the Nathan Frank Bandstand. Designed by Helfensteller, Hirsh and Watson in a classic Renaissance design, the structure was constructed of white limestone with bronze railings and rests on an island in Pagoda Lake. The pagoda was renovated in 1981 by the Central West End Charitable Trust.

Work began in August 1997 to reconstruct the lake and its Pagoda Circle, a roundabout that serves as the park's central artery. The circle has new roads, bridges, and landscaping. The lake itself is connected to nearby Angel Lake as part of the park's water system. Three bridges were constructed, one pedestrian and two vehicular, and the roads around the circle were improved, including special pavement in front of the Muny. Primary construction was completed in fall of 1999.

The Pagoda Circle also serves as the centerpiece for the generous work conducted by the Flora Conservancy, a nonprofit group that continues to help maintain the natural landscape of the park. Over a four-day period, twelve volunteer gardeners with the Conservancy, in cooperation with the Parks Department, planted more than 27,800 perennials. The landscape was designed by Oehme, van Sweden and Associates.

Today, waterfowl often greet park visitors near the lake, and the Pagoda Circle's restored grandeur is representative of the work that has gone into the park in recent years.

Jewel Box

The Jewel Box is a unique seasonal floral conservatory. It was erected by the city of St. Louis in 1936 at a cost of $117,475, with proceeds from the city and a grant from the Public Works Administration.

City engineer William C. E. Becker designed the Art Deco Jewel Box, which is on the National Register of Historic Places. The 7,500-square-foot structure stands 55 feet wide, 144 feet long, and 50 feet high and is constructed of glass and metal. The cantilevered design offsets the horizontal metal with vertical glass, supported on an arched steel frame. The modern Gothic arched steel beams resemble the branching out of mechanical tree limbs. In total, the building has 15,000 square feet of glass and is considered an engineering and design marvel. Indoor electric lights were installed in 1938 so that visitor hours could be extended.

In 2002, as a part of the Forest Park Master Plan, the Jewel Box received extensive renovations costing $3.5 million. The glass panels were cleaned, and the jungle-like profusion of trees and plants that climbed to the top of the building and obscured the light was removed, allowing sunlight to penetrate the conservatory. A new heating and cooling system was installed, and the building was cleared of asbestos and lead paint.

The interior layout was overhauled to allow for weddings and events for up to 250 people. In recent years, the Jewel Box has been a favorite location for weddings. The original design allowed visitors to see floral displays from above, while the new layouts only offers eye-level views.

The Flora Conservancy spearheaded efforts to landscape the interior and exterior of the Jewel Box. Potted and hanging plants are now arranged along the sides of the interior. Seasonal flowers, roses, lily ponds, and monuments surround the Jewel Box, with a reflecting pool mirroring the image of its entrance.

The Hadley-Dean Glass Company

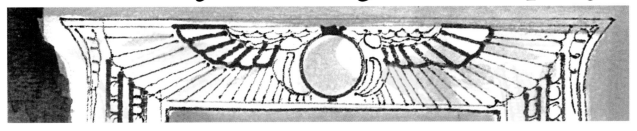

The Hadley-Dean Glass Company completed construction of its downtown office building in 1903. Isaac Taylor—chief architect of the St. Louis World's Fair—designed the neoclassical building, which is located at Eleventh and Lucas. The facade of the seven-story red-brick structure was enhanced with a brick cornice, terra cotta arched windows and lion's heads, and Bedford stone.

The glass company distributed Vitrolite, a polychrome-pigmented structural glass, along with other structural and decorative glass and tile. The material was extremely heavy, so Taylor reinforced the interior to support nearly 30 million pounds of glass. Initially, structural glass was utilitarian, but after architect Cass Gilbert used the material to decorate parts of the Woolworth Building in New York, the material became a popular replacement for marble and other materials.

In 1928 the company wanted to demonstrate the decorative potential of its product and hired Oscar Enders to design the lobby using a type of decorative glass known as Sani-Onyx. Strongly contrasting the late Victorian exterior, the lobby features an Art Deco style with an Egyptian motif.

The lobby became an instant attraction. A large sun-like disc resembling an Egyptian chandelier hung in the lobby. The floor plan resembled an Egyptian temple, with massive pylons leading into an entrance court, a hypostyle hall of lotus stalk–shaped columns, chambers, and a sanctuary.

The Hadley-Dean Glass Company went out of business in the 1970s. In 1982 many of the Egyptian motifs were removed when the building underwent needed renovations. Some of the glass displays were reincorporated and installed at a new side entrance.

Today, the building's upper stories are modernized office spaces, while the lobby floor has been renovated into a restaurant appropriately named Mosaic. The restaurant opened in 2004, and although its theme is based on decorative tiles, it has no connection to the glass company. Traces of the glorious Egyptian motif glasswork remain near and around the elevators, and a few panels can be found on the doors to the women's restroom.

Cathedral Basilica of St. Louis

Construction of the New Cathedral, designed by Barnett, Haynes & Barnett, was begun in 1907 under the governance of Cardinal John Glennon, and over one hundred years later, the building is still unfinished. Many of the details, such as the Romanesque capitals above the outside columns at the side doors, remain uncut. Green tiles cap the two square towers and the central dome. The dome, topped by a cross that rises 227 feet above street level, is the most striking exterior feature of the building.

The building itself is an excellent example of modified Byzantine architecture with Romanesque exterior features. For example, the shape of the Greek Cross floor plan closely resembles San Marco in Venice. Two small domes make up the long arm of the cross while two half domes form the transept or short arm of the cross. A central, high red dome rests on four arches that carry its weight to great piers. Seraphim are depicted in the pendentives above the piers. The columns, altars, statues, and floors have been constructed from marble from all parts of the world. Italian marble columns support the fifty-seven-foot baldachin, a small replica of the exterior dome.

An observer can feel humbled in the vastness of the interior. Nineteen hundred people can be seated comfortably within the church. The height from floor to the largest dome is 143 feet, the same as the Pantheon in Rome. The rose windows by Tiffany dominate the north and south walls.

The interior walls are decorated with the largest collection of mosaics in the Western world. A contract was made with a Berlin tile firm that sent Paul Heuduck to set up the Ravenna Mosaic Company in St. Louis to install the mosaics. Before being sent to the Ravenna Company, the materials for the mosaics were cut in a Berlin studio. During World War II, Herman Goering protected the studio. Russians stole all of the original drawings of the cathedral interior, but they are now held at the University of Warsaw.

Mosaics installed on wall panels in the narthex, or front lobby, depict the life of Louis IX, patron of St. Louis, while mosaics covering the interior domes, walls, and arches picture St. Louis history, western expansion, and biblical scenes. Mosaic installation began in 1912, and the work was completed in 1988. Nearly 43 million tiles cover more than 80,000 square feet.

Four chapels are within the basilica; two flank the nave, while two flank the choir. Three cardinals are buried in the All Souls Chapel. Their red hats hang from above, waiting to turn to dust.

Bevo Mill and Feasting Fox

For August A. Busch, Sr., the long ride home on the Gravois Road to Grant's Farm from his brewery downtown proved difficult in inclement weather. Plans for a stopping-off place to eat dinner or stay for the night took shape. He hired architects Klipstein and Rathmann to study Dutch architectural styles with the intention of building an authentic Dutch windmill. In 1915 he found a site halfway between the two destinations. Busch built Bevo Mill and the adjoining garden for family dining. He gathered stones from the farm to be used on the exterior of the building.

In 1917 Busch opened the remainder of the building as a public restaurant. When the Prohibition movement was gaining steam, he used the restaurant as a way of proving that without hard liquor family dining with beer and wine was possible. The Mill Room remained his private dining room for many years.

The Bevo Mill became a favorite family restaurant, boasting several unique architectural details. The dark wooden walls and exposed timbers in the main dining room are reminiscent of a hunting lodge. Antlers from deer, elk, and moose hang from some walls, while others are decorated with large tiled murals. The foyer and Mill Room feature vaulted ceilings with groined arches. Stone-carved gnomes—exhibited at the Paris Exposition in 1889—overlook the restaurant from the end of the arches.

In the 1980s a twenty-month restoration cost four times the original construction. The windmill blades are still operating. And with a close eye, a pair of cement storks can be seen sitting atop the chimney. These storks are German and Dutch good luck charms.

Anheuser-Busch built many restaurants within a few miles of the Bevo Mill, including the Stork Inn at the intersection of Virginia and Idaho avenues and Gretchen's Inn at Grand and Meramec avenues. Busch built these restaurants to counteract the growing Prohibition movement. High license fees forced many restaurateurs out of business, so Anheuser-Busch bought these properties and paid the fees while the proprietors ran the restaurants, making sure they served plenty of A-B products.

Gretchen's Inn's timber and stucco construction, steeply pitched roof, and corner turret have made it a historic landmark. Under the name of Al Smith's, the restaurant operated from the 1930s to 1961, when Fred and Evelyn Krumm—who had been managing the restaurant since 1945—took the reins.

The building was extensively rehabbed after a fire in 1968. In 1986 the restaurant went out of business, and the building remained vacant for eight years. Antique collectors and neighborhood residents Sue and Marty Luepker saved the landmark from demolition and restored it to its original splendor and renamed it the Feasating Fox. They restored, revived, and filled the historical building with St. Louis memorabilia. Beautiful leaded-glass windows abound. The rich interior decor brings Bavarian Old World charm back to a once German-dominated area of the city.

Masonic Temple

The Masonic Temple is one of St. Louis's most picturesque buildings—a Parthenon-like structure lifted fourteen stories into the sky. Its facades, either windowless or with relatively miniscule cut openings, give it an appearance of massiveness, permanence, and impenetrability. It is built of steel encased in concrete and contains over 6 million cubic feet of space.

With a budget of $4 million, architects Thomas Young and Albert Groves of Eames & Young set out to create a stone monument that would incorporate the temples of ancient Babylon, mighty Egypt, and Classical Greece. Their designs were based on the concept that all temples are built on high terraces. The three receding stages of the classic-style building are symbolic of the three gigantic monumental flights of steps in achieving Masonry. The massive structure rises to a height of 185 feet and is faced with Bedford limestone and gray Chelmsford granite trim. The front of the building showcases two sets of Ionic columns.

The building was dedicated on October 26, 1926, and construction was funded solely by donations from the twenty-five thousand Missouri Masons. The lodge was organized by twelve St. Louis members in May 1872.

Details and symbolism abound on the building's exterior. From the top down, highlights include a relief sculpture of the Greek god Mercury within the temple pediment. Balustrades with moldings were used instead of cornices. Bronze discs decorate the second tier and represent shields of the vanquished captured in war. The symbol of the Masons—the square and compass—bookends the lower columns. Impressive bronze doors rest behind the lower columns as they overlook a large flight of steps that leads down to Lindell Boulevard. Sphinxes stand as sentinels on either side of the doors. Two Latin inscriptions are etched on the front of the temple: "Let there be light and there was light" and "To the glory of the great architect of the universe and the brotherhood of man."

The interior of the temple is lavish. Marble flooring and ornaments complement stained glass windows, original walnut furniture, and art and statuary. The main lobby contains the only known statue of President George Washington in Masonic attire. A 2,200-seat theater space on the first floor is still unfinished.

Fox Theatre

In 1929 William Fox, founder of 20th Century Fox, built this extravagant St. Louis movie house to show his films. The theatre was built on the site of the Grand Avenue Presbyterian Church, which had been empty since 1914. Detroit-based architect C. Howard Crane designed the theatre in a Siamese Byzantine style at a cost of $6 million. Construction took only a year and a half. Countless artisans and workers brought the theatre to life.

Architectural sculptor Victor Berlendis supervised the creation of the ornamental plaster interiors. Berlendis supervised, sculpted, and designed a number of buildings in the city, including the Steedman Room in the Central Library, the Ambassador Theatre on Seventh Street, the Kiel Opera House, and many private homes in the Central West End.

The lobby of the Fox was designed to overwhelm, and it succeeded. It was constructed to resemble an Indian Buddhist monastery, with a deep red and gold carpet and rows of red columns on the flanks. A pair of golden griffins stood sentinel at the grand stairway. Construction was supervised by the Aronberg-Fried Company, which was brought in by Fox. The ornamental exterior of the building is terra cotta, created by Winkle Terra Cotta Company. Arabesque lattices, Egyptian pillars, cloisonné elephants, stained glass, polished brass fixtures, and other ornamentations filled the Fox.

In the late 1920s, William Fox built a number of movie palaces across the country to play his studio's films. Many of these theatres were demolished; others were restored. Thankfully, St. Louis's Fox Theatre was brought back to life.

William Fox lost his fortune in the stock market crash, making his grasp on his theatre chain tenuous. Fanchon and Marco took ownership of the theatre in 1934. Throughout the middle decades of the twentieth century, the Fox Theatre was operated by Arthur Enterprises and hosted a variety of movies, concerts, festivals, pageants, and conventions. Arthur Enterprises, however, was forced to close the doors in 1978.

The company Fox Associates, which included Mary Strauss and her husband, Leon, bought the building and brought the theatre back to life by reopening the doors in 1982. With $2 million-plus invested, they restored the theater to its original magnificence. The task was daunting; the ornate theatre was in decrepit condition. The 18-foot-wide, 2,000-pound, 480-bulb chandelier was lowered and cleaned, and all 4,500 seats were removed, cleaned, and repaired. New carpets were installed. Plasterwork and art glass were re-created and installed. Light fixtures were replaced. State-of-the-art sound and lighting were installed. The work was endless.

Concerts, musicals, films, and events take the stage today. After a stage expansion, the Fox has brought Broadway to St. Louis.

Soulard Market

During the 1830s, population expansion occurred rapidly to the south of St. Louis. French families developed country estates. In the following decades, many Central European immigrants settled in the area and needed a place to buy produce.

On June 21, 1838, Julia Cerre Soulard, widow of St. Louis's surveyor general under the Spanish regime, reserved an area of two city blocks to be used as a public market. She eventually sold this farm meadow in 1841 to the city with the stipulation that it remain a public market. The market is located at Lafayette and Seventh streets.

In 1843 farmers and vendors sold shares to raise money for a one-story brick building, which, as today, housed perishable goods, while produce was sold on the exterior. The most famous farmer to sell goods there was Ulysses S. Grant, who sold cordwood cut from his farm, Hardscrabble. As the Civil War took Grant away from the farm, it brought the Home Guard to the market. The Home Guard consisted of German pro-Union forces, and they used the market land—which was just a few blocks from the U.S. Arsenal—as an encampment.

After a series of post–Civil War expansions, Soulard Market was hit by the tornado of 1896. Like much of Soulard, Lafayette Square, and downtown, the Soulard Market was heavily damaged by the storm. Most notably, a second-story addition was laid to waste.

In 1923, St. Louisans approved an unprecedented bond issue—$87.4 million worth of city improvements, the largest of its kind in an American city. A new Soulard Market was one of these improvements. The present Soulard Market was erected in 1929. City architect Albert A. Osburg used an Italian Renaissance style, which is similar to the 1419 Florentine Foundling Hospital designed by the Renaissance sculptor and architect Filippo Brunelleschi.

The two-story brick structure is at the apex of the market, with an all-purpose gymnasium on the second floor. Two covered aisles extend both to the east and to the west, each a city block long. Produce vendors sell their goods in this open-air venue, while vendors of perishable goods remain on the first floor of the central building.

Soulard Farmer's Market is one of the oldest public markets still in existence in the United States. It is the lone functioning survivor in the city of the many public markets. Visitors regularly browse the stalls of local farmers for fresh picked vegetables, live poultry, fresh fish, meats, cheeses, bakery goods, and seasonal flowers. Many of the vendors have been selling at the market for several generations.

Civil Courts

The thirteen-story Civil Courts Building was the cornerstone of the $87.4 million bond issue that passed in 1923. Citizens passed the bond issue—intended to improve the public buildings in the city—passed by a 4–1 margin, and it was the largest of its kind in any American city.

St. Louis hired architects Ernest Klipstein and Walter Rathmann to design the new courthouse. Klipstein and Rathmann designed a number of unique buildings in the St. Louis region, notably a handful of Anheuser-Busch's most prominent taverns, the Bevo Mill, the Stork Inn, and Gretchen's Inn; the Bauernhof at the present-day Grant's Farm; the U.S. Post Office on Eighteenth and Market; the Eastman Kodak Building at 1009 Olive; and the Gorlock Building at 101 W. Lockwood.

Klipstein and Rathmann were members of the Plaza Commission, which was a group of architects and engineers assigned to oversee the construction of Memorial Plaza, of which the Civil Courts Building was a part.

The Civil Courts Building is Klipstein and Rathmann's most notable addition to St. Louis's skyline. They aimed high with the design and modeled it after one of the Seven Wonders of the Ancient World: the Mausoleum of King Mausolus at Halicarnassus. The cost exceeded $4.5 million.

The building is a combination of Greek and Egyptian styles, and it was constructed of Bedford limestone. When construction was completed in 1930, the Civil Courts Building was the tallest structure in the city of St. Louis, standing at 386 feet.

The re-creation of the mausoleum makes up the top three floors of the building. An aluminum, stepped pyramid caps off the temple, which is surrounded by Ionic columns, eight to a side. A law library rests behind the columns, and an observation promenade offers sweeping views of the city. Two cast-aluminum sphinx-like griffins sit atop the pyramid surveying the city. They represent mercy and justice.

Santa Maria

"A full-sized replica of the flagship of Christopher Columbus' discovery fleet is moored at the end of a 15th Century-style floating Spanish wharf. Termed by the exhibitors "Space Ship – 1492," this Santa Maria is the product of a distinguished intercontinental collaboration that insured authenticity."

—Description of the ship at the Spanish Pavilion in New York City

Alfonso J. Cervantes served as mayor of St. Louis from 1965 to 1973. He expertly steered the city of St. Louis through a turbulent time for the nation by focusing on race relations, city finances, and crime prevention. A minor blemish on his track record came to be known as Cervantes' Folly.

In 1964 and 1965 New York City hosted the World's Fair, and many thought the Spanish Pavilion was the most attractive building at the fair. Cervantes, being of Spanish decent, celebrated St. Louis's Spanish heritage by purchasing the pavilion and an exact replica of Christopher Columbus's *Santa Maria*.

The pavilion was reconstructed just north of the new Busch Stadium. The building failed as a tourist attraction, as it left visitors with little to see or do. Less than fifteen years after it was rebuilt, developers built the Mariott Pavilion Hotel over it.

The *Santa Maria* replica was purchased and brought to St. Louis as a riverfront tourist attraction. Moored at the base of the Gateway Arch, the ship, like the Spanish Pavilion, lacked crowds, but unlike the pavilion, the *Santa Maria* didn't find a happy ending.

The galleon was built in Barcelona in 1963 specifically for the New York World's Fair. The construction not only held true to the technology and material of the thirteenth century, but the ship reached the New World with fifteenth-century techniques as well. A crew sailed the ship to New York and dealt with the same obstacles as Columbus's crew. The replica had to face one obstacle, however, that the original didn't have to face the Mighty Mississippi.

The *Santa Maria* was involved in a number of accidents on the Mississippi River, but it was finally done in by a barge. A river barge knocked the replica from its moorings, and the ship floated unmanned into a series of other barges, then sank. It was salvaged, restored, and relocated to the coast of Florida, where it promptly caught fire and sank for good.

Busch Stadium

There have been three incarnations of Busch Stadium. The first was Sportsman's Park. After Anheuser-Busch bought the Cardinals—and the stadium—in 1953, the company renamed the ballpark Busch Stadium. The second Busch Stadium is now referred to as Busch Memorial Stadium and was used from 1966 until the present-day Busch Stadium opened in 2006.

Busch Memorial was a multipurpose stadium constructed in the heart of downtown St. Louis with the hopes of bringing people—and business—back to the region's hub. Busch officially opened on May 12, 1966, when the St. Louis Cardinals defeated the Atlanta Braves in twelve innings. For the next thirty-eight years, the stadium hosted St. Louis Cardinals baseball, St. Louis Cardinals football, concerts, and events. The maximum capacity was 50,345.

The stadium opened a year after the completion of the Gateway Arch, and the ballfield's design complemented the monument. Designed by world-famous architect Edward Durrell Stone—who also created Radio City Music Hall and the Museum of Modern Art, among other U.S. landmarks—Busch Stadium was a Modernist interpretation of the Roman Coliseum. The circular structure was eight hundred feet in diameter and was crowned with a series of ninety-six arches. Built of concrete, the shell of the utilitarian Busch Stadium was primarily transparent, as passers-by were able to see the walking ramps teeming with fans wearing Cardinal red.

St. Louis baseball was wildly successful during the thirty-eight years in Busch Memorial Stadium, winning six National League pennants and two World Championships. The final game in the stadium was played on October 19, 2005, with the Cardinals losing the pennant to division rival Houston Astros.

The Big Red, St. Louis's football franchise from 1960 to 1987, likewise moved from the old Busch Stadium at Grand and Dodier and first played at Busch Memorial in 1966. The Big Red played twenty-two seasons in Busch before moving to Arizona. Although the team made the playoffs three times in their tenure at Busch, they never hosted a playoff game.

Old Cathedral

The first mass celebrated in St. Louis occurred in 1764, the year Pierre Laclede founded the trading post. Laclede set aside land for a church and graveyard, which is where the first mass was held. This land is the current site of the Basilica of St. Louis, or Old Cathedral.

The Old Cathedral is the fourth church built in St. Louis. The first two churches were made of logs; the third of bricks. The first, constructed in 1770, lasted only six years. In 1772 the lieutenant governor of the Spanish-run territory, Don Pedro Piernos, donated a sanctuary bell, which remains onsite in an attached museum. The second log church was built in 1776 and was paid for in deerskin, a common currency in the city's early years. The third brick building was constructed in 1818–1820.

St. Louis became a diocese of the Catholic Church in 1826, and a permanent church became necessary. Joseph Rosati was appointed as the first bishop of the Diocese of St. Louis, and he immediately set forth a plan to construct a cathedral. Construction began on the first cathedral west of the Mississippi in 1831, and work was completed in 1834. Bishop Rosati is buried beneath the cathedral's sanctuary.

The Old Cathedral, as it has been known since the New Cathedral was constructed in the early 1900s, is a Greek Revival building. Architects Joseph Laveille and George Morton of Laveille and Morton designed the church. Some of their other works include buildings at Jefferson Barracks and the original courthouse, which was incorporated into the Old Courthouse.

The front of the stone cathedral is constructed of limestone with four Doric columns holding up the pediment of the portico. Three doors at the main entrance symbolize the trinity. The same inscription is above each door but in three different languages; from left to right, it is written in French, Latin, and English. The inscription states: "My house shall be called the house of prayer."

The Old Cathedral has endured, despite destruction that brought down all of the buildings surrounding it. It first survived the Great Fire of 1849. Then, more than a century later, it survived the demolition of forty square blocks to make room for the Gateway Arch. In fact, it was the only building spared.

Eads Bridge

The Eads Bridge, possibly St. Louis's most significant architectural contribution, was designed by a riverboat contractor and salvager with no formal architectural or engineering training: James B. Eads. This lack of formal education may be the reason why the bridge, which was considered impossible to build, was completed.

Construction began on the bridge in 1867 and lasted seven years, with its dedication on July 4, 1874. At the time, the Eads Bridge was the longest bridge in the world, with a length of 6,442 feet. Three arches—with respective spans of 500, 520, and 500 feet—are held by four granite piers.

The Eads Bridge was the first of its kind in many ways: It was the first major bridge to use chrome steel as its primary structural component; it was the first to use cantilevered construction; and it was the first to use pneumatic caissons to construct its piers. The steel and cantilevered construction gave an unprecedented strength to the bridge, which was needed to allow river traffic to continue beneath the arches. The bridge's caissons remain some of the deepest ever sunk. Fifteen people died while constructing the bridge, with scores more injured, most by caisson disease, or "the bends."

The Eads Bridge was constructed to connect the St. Louis rail yards to the eastern markets and to compete against the burgeoning Chicago as a hub. Although the bridge was an engineering marvel, the utilitarian logistics were not in place for the bridge to serve its purpose. Rail lines were not properly coordinated with the bridge on the Illinois side. The bridge, which cost $10 million to construct, proved a financial disaster for the St. Louis Merchants Exchange. Railroad companies were pressured by politicians and businesses alike to boycott the bridge and continue to use ferryboats to transport railcars across the river.

In 1881, railroad magnate Jay Gould bought the bridge at a fraction of the construction cost. By the late 1880s, many of the logistic problems were solved, and costly levies were lifted.

The bridge served rail traffic steadily until 1974. Nineteen years later, the region's MetroLink light rail system re-established rail traffic on the bridge, with vehicle and pedestrian traffic remaining on the upper level.

Private Places

St. Louis embraced the notion of the "private place," where residents actually own the street and sidewalks and are responsible for maintenance. St. Louis's private streets are lined with grandiose homes and ornate entry gates, many of which can be closed at either end to restrict traffic flow.

In the nineteenth century, St. Louis was a compact, polluted, and bustling city, and those who could afford large homes away from the congestion moved away. Some had large country estates, while others tended to congregate. Although a public street, Lucas Place, created in 1850 by banker and land developer James H. Lucas, set a precedent for future private places by establishing deed restrictions. The real estate market boomed in the mid-1800s, affording extravagant homes equipped with ballrooms, running water, and gas lighting. Lucas Place was located on today's Locust Street between Thirteenth and Jefferson, and Missouri Park served as a buffer between the private street and the city. The Campbell House Museum—at Fifteenth and Locust—is a remnant of Lucas Place.

The most fashionable private places moved steadily westward as transportation improved and the city grew. In 1867, Benton Place in the Lafayette Square neighborhood began the trend and was the first street to give total responsibility of landscaping, lighting, and road and sewer maintenance and repair to the residents. Victorian architecture dominated Benton Place and the neighborhood at large.

Vandeventer Place—the present site of the Veterans Administration Hospital on Grand Boulevard—was home to the social and business elite at the end of the nineteenth century. Julius Pitzman, who designed Benton Place, also created Vandeventer Place, where various renowned architects designed the mansions. Memories of the downfall of Lucas Place were alive and well with the residents of Vandeventer Place, but the fashionable neighborhood was eventually demolished to make way for the hospital.

Shaw Place was another Victorian private street. Henry Shaw hired architect George Barnett to re-create a ten-house, oval, private street that he remembered from his childhood in his native England. Shaw's intent was to set a standard for houses built around his botanical garden. The ploy worked. The adjacent Flora Place remains the backbone of today's Shaw Neighborhood.

Private places still thrive in St. Louis, with the most elegant in St. Louis's Central West End neighborhood. Noteworthy streets include Westmoreland Place, Portland Place, Washington Terrace, and Kingsbury Place, which were developed at the turn of the twentieth century.

Wainwright Building

In 1891 Louis Sullivan and Dankmar Adler designed the Wainwright Building at the corner of Chestnut and Seventh streets in downtown St. Louis. The Wainwright Building is among the first skyscrapers constructed. The building was erected for local businessman Ellis Wainwright, and the design greatly advanced American architecture and placed Sullivan at the head of the modern movement. Sullivan mentored Frank Lloyd Wright, who worked in Sullivan's office from 1888 to 1893, during the construction of the Wainwright Building.

The technical advances used in the construction of the Wainwright Building add to its significance. Most notably, a steel frame was used, replacing the heavy masonry of load-bearing walls used for taller building of the day. The steel frame became the basis of the skyscrapers that later dominated the skylines of U.S. cities. Because of the use of electricity and ventilating systems, and the development of the elevator by Elisha Otis, Sullivan and other architects were able to increase the height of buildings.

The overall design of the Wainwright Building was based on a column, with a base, shaft, and capital. The base is made up of the first two floors, which have little ornamentation and consist of brown sandstone atop granite. The shaft includes floors two through nine. Vertical brick columns emphasize the building's height, and intricate terra cotta designs enhance the otherwise sheer and uninterrupted exterior. The capital, or top floor, is an elaborate terra cotta cornice.

In 1968, the Wainwright became a National Historic Landmark. The building was rescued from disrepair by the State of Missouri in the 1970s. State offices still occupy the building.

Title Guaranty and Buder Buildings

The Wainwright Building is the last remnant of Real Estate Row, a lineup of skyscrapers that dominated St. Louis's skyline for years. The Buder and Title Guaranty Buildings made up the rest of Real Estate Row and were demolished in the 1980s. The loss of these buildings is one of the biggest architectural tragedies in St. Louis.

Originally known as the Missouri Pacific Building, the twelve-story Buder Building was located at the intersection of Seventh and Market. It was one of seven buildings constructed along Seventh Street after the completion of the Wainwright Building in time for the 1904 World's Fair (Buder, Title Guaranty, DeMenil, Fullerton, Holland, Union Trust, and Mercantile Buildings). Built in the Beaux Arts/Renaissance Revival style for $600,000 in 1901 by Architect W. Albert Swasey, the exterior buff brick was overlaid by ornate terra cotta ornamentation, which was provided by St. Louis's Winkle Terra Cotta Company.

The Title Guaranty Building, originally known as the Lincoln Trust Building, was constructed in 1898 at 706 Chestnut and designed by William Eames and Thomas Young. St. Louisans Eames and Young teamed up to design a large number of important buildings across the nation, including the U.S. Customs House in San Francisco. Some contributions to St. Louis included the Cupples Station warehouses, the International (Liggett) Building, and a large number of residences in the area's private places. Eames also designed the Bissell Water Tower. The Title Guaranty Building was considered by many to be the best of Eames and Young's tall office buildings.

The Title Guaranty Building consisted of two thirteen-story towers connected by a one-story entrance to make an "H" shape. Like the Wainwright and Buder Buildings, the Title's towers were made of three parts—base, shaft, and capital—and used vertical brick columns to accentuate the building's height. Ornate terra cotta dressed the exterior of the shaft and the capital.

St. Louis's Winkle Terra Cotta Company provided the detailed terra cotta work here as well. Salvaged terra cotta is all that remains of the Buder and Title Buildings. Museums across the city house and display the collection, including the Sheldon Art Galleries. Both buildings were on the National Register of Historic Places and were well occupied when they were demolished.

M. Bradley

Goldenrod Showboat

Built in 1909 for W. R. Markle by the Pope Dock Company at Parkersburg, West Virginia, the *Goldenrod Showboat* was the last theater boat constructed for the Mississippi entertainment trade. It was also the largest, at two hundred feet by forty-five feet. Showboats by design were not self-powered, and the *Goldenrod* was towed often in its history.

The Gothic, steel-hulled vessel operated in fifteen states. River-town residents eagerly awaited the ship's arrival, along with its professional entertainment shows. Captain J. William Menke, who purchased "the world's largest and greatest showboat" in 1922, was largely responsible for the touring. The tours inspired many, possibly even Edna Ferber, the author of the book, *Showboat*, which became the basis of Jerome Kern's musical. The touring came to a halt in 1937.

The *Goldenrod* found a "permanent" home on the St. Louis riverfront at the Locust Street Landing. The *Goldenrod*'s theater sat nearly fourteen hundred people, and the ornate interior—gilt, red draperies, friezes, and full-length mirrors—was accentuated by more than twenty-five hundred lights. Although the ship slowly deteriorated at the St. Louis levee, entertainment continued. The ship became a staging ground for up-and-coming entertainers of all sorts, and the riverboat hosted the St. Louis Ragtime Festival.

In 1988 the city of St. Charles purchased the *Goldenrod*—a National Historic Landmark since December 1967. Moored at St. Charles's Frontier Park on the Missouri River, the ship caught another wind and was elegantly restored. Dinner theater and other live shows entertained large crowds until March 2000.

In January 2002, a logjam bashed in the hull. After repairs, a new owner relocated the ship to the Illinois River north of Harden, Illinois. The vessel is now in dry dock at Kampsville, Illinois.

The Arena

Just west of the Forest Park Highlands—a St. Louis amusement park—St. Louis industrialist Ben Brinkman and the Chamber of Commerce erected the St. Louis Arena in 1929 for $2 million. The Arena was slated to host the annual National Dairy Show, a major source of revenue that immediately came to a halt with the onset of the Great Depression.

St. Louis was left with a seventeen-thousand-seat arena and little to show. The structure was innovative and immense. Covering a quarter-acre of land, it was exceeded in size only by New York's Madison Square Garden. Architect Gustel Kiewitt created the domed structure with a roof-spanning process known as lamella design. Lamella roofs were developed in Germany in 1908 and gained popularity in the 1920s and 1930s. The technique fell out of favor after World War II after a few notable lamella roofs collapsed. The Arena's design involved twenty steel cantilever trusses that supported a central section of arched timber. The space between cantilevers measured 155 feet, and it was one of the largest lamella roofs ever created. Although the roof to the Arena stood the test of time, a tornado took off a tower in 1959.

From the 1930s to 1967, the Arena hosted a number of sporting events, circuses, and expositions and did not find a permanent resident until Sid Salomon, Jr., bought the building and brought the St. Louis Blues and professional ice hockey to St. Louis. Salomon purchased the Arena for $4 million in 1967. Ralston Purina bought out Salomon in 1977, and the building was known as the Checkerdome until 1983.

The Arena closed its doors in 1993 when the Blues relocated to the Kiel Center downtown. The Arena's future was left in doubt. Many ideas were hatched, including incorporating the Old Barn into Forest Park as a new city aquarium or as part of one of the existing museums. No idea came to fruition, and on the evening of February 27, 1999, thousands of St. Louisans gathered to witness the end of a beloved building, as the Arena was imploded—a spectacle that took only thirty seconds.

SS Admiral

The SS *Admiral* was originally named the *Albatross*. The *Albatross* was constructed in 1907 by Dubuque Boat and Boiler Company for the Louisiana and Mississippi Valley Transfer Company, which used the ship to ferry railcars across the Mississippi River at the St. Louis riverfront.

The *Albatross*'s exterior in no way resembled the present-day *Admiral*. The ship went through a series of renovations, additions, and overhauls, beginning in 1920. Ripley Boat Company purchased the ship and converted it into the largest passenger riverboat in the United States, with a length greater than 360 feet.

In 1937 the Streckfus Steamer Company purchased the *Albatross* for $1 million. The Streckfus brothers held a fleet of excursion riverboats in St. Louis and New Orleans that toured the Mississippi River. They hired the best jazz performers of the era to entertain, led by Fate Marable, Singleton Palmer, and Louis Armstrong. The Streckfus brothers excursion boats went a long way toward developing jazz music.

In 1940 the ship underwent another series of extensive conversions. This time, the end result warranted a new name, since, other than the steel hull and steam boilers, the ship was fully unrecognizable as the *Albatross*. The five steel Art Deco decks of the new SS *Admiral* were a marvel. With a 4,400-passenger capacity, the *Admiral* was the largest passenger riverboat in the world. The new excursion ship was an entertainment paradise, with shows, dancing, and restaurants.

By the 1970s the *Admiral* had fallen into disrepair. An organization called the SS Admiral Partners bought the ship and gave her a major makeover, including removing the engines. The SS Admiral Partners returned grand entertainment to the beloved, now permanently moored ship. The restaurants, nightclubs, and live shows lasted only a decade, before casinos took the wheel. The President Casino on the Admiral has been in operation since the mid-1990s.

Coral Court

One mile west of the St. Louis city limits, the glazed tile motor court hotel stood along Route 66. Designed in the 1940s Streamline Moderne style—the final phase of Art Deco—Coral Court was the finest example of the early style of a motor hotel. The decor remained the same to the end of its days as if time stood still: Doors inside a heated garage led into a room furnished with a red shag rug, tiled bathroom, block glass windows, hot-water radiant heat, 1970s TV, AM radio, and double bed.

In 1941, John H. Carr planned to build ten two-room cabins and a central building at a cost of seven thousand dollars. St. Louis architect Adolph L. Struebig was hired to build Carr's vision of the best maintenance-free motel in St. Louis. Struebig designed individual units with flat roofs, honey-yellow glazed tile with reddish brown trim, and eight-inch-square glass blocks.

In 1946, Carr added additional units and hired Harold Tyrer to design them. These units had a bay area at the entrance that contained a Murphy bed. Because of the two glass brick rounded bays, these rooms were called "Mae West" units.

To roadside fans, Coral Court was a shrine. The rooms could be rented by the hour. The final additions to the no-tell motel took place in 1953 when Tyrer designed two-story units that housed eight rooms. Three such units were built in the back of the property. A pool was also added in the early 1960s. Behind the entrance's stone gates electric eyes announced the arrival of a customer. An open garage would be ready for the client to drive in.

In 1953, the scandal of the Bobby Greenlease kidnapping extended to Coral Court. Carl Austin Hall and Bonny Brown Heady abducted the son of a millionaire car dealer. They killed the boy and hid out in St. Louis. Hall spent one evening hiding out at the Coral Court. The ransom amount was $600,000, the largest paid up to that point in U.S. history. Only about half of the money was ever recovered.

John Carr died in 1984 and left the Coral Court to his widow. In 1987, she tried to sell the motel to a developer who wanted to build a strip mall. The buildings deteriorated, with nothing reinvested for the upkeep. Preservationists continued to work hard to save the Coral Court from destruction. In 1989, the Coral Court was accepted onto the National Register of Historic Places, but this act failed to save the cluster of buildings. The motel was finally closed in 1993.

The village of Marlborough re-zoned the property and called for condemnation of the buildings. Demolition of Coral Courts was done during the summer of 1995.

A quiet subdivision was built behind the remaining stone fence and entryway.

The Parkmoor

Sandwiches
ALL CREAM ICE CREAM

FRIED CHICKEN   STEAKS SANDWICH

Parkmoor

In 1924 William Louis McGinley and his brother designed a service food tray for cars. They applied for a patent for the "auto service tray," which they named TraCo. The trays fit every model of car, and they were lightweight, large enough to hold two dinners, and they stacked for easy storage. McGinley wrote brochures on how to build a profitable curb-service business, and he traveled the country teaching about curb-service businesses and promoting his tray.

In 1930 the Parkmoor Restaurant opened at the intersection of Big Bend and Clayton. The restaurant ushered in the nationwide carhop and drive-in culture as the first in St. Louis to offer curb-service dining.

The Parkmoor was known for good, fresh food at fair prices, with the chickburger—a specially made ground chicken sandwich—serving as the trademark entree. Homemade ice cream lured diners from throughout the St. Louis region. Parkmoor employees were noted for their crisp uniforms, smiles, and adept tray service.

At the zenith of curb service, McGinley had seven Parkmoor locations, and there were two incarnations at Clayton and Big Bend. The original drive-in was replaced by a diner in the 1970s. The new building was an example of the unofficial Coffee Shop Modern architectural style.

For sixty years, the Parkmoor bridged surrounding neighborhoods: upper-middle-class residents from University City and Clayton; students from Washington University; teens from throughout the St. Louis area; and families and individuals from all walks of life.

In the fall of 1999 Lou Ellen McGinley, William's daughter, closed the Parkmoor's doors forever.

Ted Drewes

Ted Drewes Frozen Custard is a St. Louis tradition that originated in Florida. Ted Drewes, Sr., brought his frozen custard to St. Louis in 1930 and opened a stand on Natural Bridge. In just over a decade, Ted Drewes expanded to two additional locations: the first, on South Grand Avenue, opened in 1931, and the famous Chippewa location opened in 1941. In 1958 the original St. Louis location shut its doors, and Ted Drewes has been content with the brisk business at its two South St. Louis locations.

Located along historic Route 66, the Chippewa location is the crown jewel, with crowds typically bordering on the surreal. When established in 1941, the Chippewa location was on the southwest edge of town, at the western edge of the just-forming St. Louis Hills neighborhood. The lightbulb-studded arrow was once necessary to lure in customers beneath the building's icicle-covered eaves.

Frozen custard is more dense than ice cream. Less air is allowed into the product during its production. Also, frozen custard is made with eggs and butterfat, in addition to the standard ice cream ingredients. The concrete was introduced at Ted Drewes in 1959. A customer wanted a thicker shake, and Ted Drewes offered him one so thick that he could hold it upside down.

Ted Drewes, Jr., still operates his frozen custard stands and can be found serving up his famous concrete.

White Castle

White Castle is the oldest fast-food hamburger chain in America. Edgar Waldo "Billy" Ingram and Walter Anderson opened a five-stool burger stand in Wichita, Kansas, in 1921. The partners quickly branched out, with multiple restaurants in Wichita, and by the mid-1920s they had expanded to other midwestern cities.

Lloyd Ray, a White Castle employee, designed the prefabricated white porcelain enamel exteriors that helped make the restaurant chain so well known. The design was modeled after Chicago's Water Tower. The prefab building measured twenty-eight feet by twenty-eight feet, and the design included stained glass windows, a parapet wall, crenellated towers, and octagonal buttresses. From 1928 to 1955, White Castle manufactured fifty-five numbered restaurants in the Midwest and the East with Ray's design.

In 1931 White Castle pioneered the newspaper coupon, and its venture was tested on the St. Louis market. Using the "Buy 'em by the sack" marketing campaign, the coupon offered five hamburgers for ten cents. The coupon was a major success.

Six years after White Castle introduced the newspaper coupon, restaurant number 24 was constructed at the intersection of Hampton and Chippewa in South St. Louis. Few original buildings remain; the White Castle number 24 is among those that did not survive.

White Castle number 24 closed in 1982. The only room to eat was at a small counter with low round stools, and the eatery was mainly a carry-out restaurant along the old Route 66. Rust had overtaken the structure, which necessitated its demolition. It was torn down and replaced by a drive-in Fox Photoshop. Today, it is a Target parking lot.

Lambert Airport

St. Louis has played a leading role in American aviation history, and many of the events took place at Lambert Airport or involved its namesake, Major Albert Bond Lambert.

Lambert, president of a major pharmaceutical company in St. Louis, had the time and money to invest into a hobby of aeronautics. He was first bitten by the flying bug after taking flight with Orville Wright. Lambert became the first St. Louisan to obtain a private pilot's license. In 1907 Lambert established the St. Louis Aero Club, which created St. Louis's first airfield. In 1920 Lambert purchased a second airfield, which is today's Lambert St. Louis International Airport. The field had previously served as a balloon launch location.

In 1927 Lambert and seven other backers enabled Charles Lindbergh to embark on his record-breaking flight to Paris. One year later, after Lambert sold his airfield to the city of St. Louis, Lambert Airport became the first municipally owned airport in the nation.

Following World War II, the city of St. Louis commissioned architect Minoru Yamasaki, of Hellmuth, Yamasaki and Leinweber, to design a main terminal for the airport. Yamasaki was one of the most prominent architects of the twentieth century and a master of Romanticized Modernism. The Lambert design inspired airport design for years to come, including Eero Saarinen's TWA Terminal at New York's John F. Kennedy International Airport and Paris's Charles de Gaulle Airport.

Lambert was completed in 1956, just one year after Hellmuth, Yamasaki, and Leinweber finished work on the Pruitt-Igoe housing project. Yamasaki's buildings are known the world over, and his most famous design was the World Trade Center in New York City. George Hellmuth was the St. Louis–based partner of the firm. After the firm dissolved due to Yamasaki's health problems, Hellmuth, chief designer Gyo Obata, and head of production George Kassabaum, formed Hellmuth, Obata and Kassabaum in 1955.

Lambert's main terminal, the first of its kind in the United States, consisted of three thin shell cross vaults, with a fourth added later. Each copper vault measures 32 by 120 feet, and each contains a thirteen-foot triangular overhang. The original building had three vaults, with a fourth added in the 1970s.

Climatron

The Climatron was the first climate-controlled display-research greenhouse built inside a geodesic dome. Opened in 1960, the Climatron serves as the centerpiece to the world-renowned Missouri Botanical Garden.

The geodesic dome was developed by R. Buckminster Fuller, and it consists of a part of a sphere that is constructed of a network of triangles. The interlocking, lightweight aluminum exoskeleton helps distribute the weight of the structure, and currently, 2,425 glass panels are found within the network of triangles. St. Louis–based architectural firm the Christner Group designed the Climatron, which has a diameter of 175 feet and stands 70 feet high. The dome has no support columns, allowing for more than a half-acre of uninterrupted space.

The Climatron underwent its only renovation in 1988. In an attempt to retain the character and historical value of the original structure, a new dome was created just inside the original. Both domes contain an aluminum exoskeleton, but the new dome used glass panels rather than Plexiglas, due to the durability of glass. The original Plexiglas panels were removed.

Developed to house tropical rainforest plants, the Climatron contains more than fifteen hundred species of plants, as well as birds, animals, and fish, to give visitors a unique insight to tropical wildlife. The Climatron replaced the Palm House, which was built in 1910 on the same site.

The Planetarium

The James S. McDonnell Planetarium is located in the southeast corner of Forest Park. The city of St. Louis built the Planetarium in 1963 with funds from a 1955 bond issue and a contribution from McDonnell Douglas, a St. Louis–based aerospace manufacturer that later merged with Boeing.

Gyo Obata of the St. Louis design firm Hellmuth, Obata and Kassabaum designed the building from a concept by HOK architect Chih-Chen Jen. The design is a mathematically pure three-dimensional hyperboloid structure. The exterior of the building is made up of thin-shell reinforced concrete and is similar in appearance to a nuclear power plant.

In 1984, the Saint Louis Science Center purchased the Planetarium from the city of St. Louis. The Science Center initiated a $3.2 million renovation, which later included a pedestrian bridge over Interstate 64 connecting the Planetarium to the main building on Oakland Avenue.

One of the nation's leading aerospace education facilities, the Planetarium's remodeled interior features myriad exhibits and programs that incorporate scientific research and illustrate the past, present, and future of space travel. Highlights include a two-story Boeing Space Station; a full-size replica of SpaceShipOne, which won the Ansari X Prize; a flight simulator; and the Zeiss Mark IX projector. The Zeiss projector—one of only four in the world—displays nine-thousand-plus stars on an eighty-foot dome in the Orthwein Star Bay in the heart of the Planetarium. Other features of the projector include moving the sky ten thousand years in time, both forward and backward; demonstrating celestial phenomena; and offering celestial viewpoints from other planets.

Gateway Arch

The Gateway Arch is one of the most recognizable structures in the United States, if not the world. Standing 630 feet (sixty-two stories), the Arch is a catenary curve, the basis of which is a chain held in the middle with its ends hanging freely. The Arch's legs stand 630 feet apart.

St. Louis booster Luther Ely Smith conceived of a contest to select a national monument to Thomas Jefferson in the mid-1930s. Architect Eero Saarinen won on February 14, 1948, with his catenary curve design. By the early 1940s, forty square blocks of the St. Louis riverfront were cleared to make room for the national park and monument. The chosen land was essentially the original platted land for St. Louis when it was a trading post in the eighteenth century. Many historic and significant buildings were razed.

Construction on the Arch was delayed until February 12, 1963, nearly two years after Saarinen passed away. Construction took just two and a half years, and the final section was placed on October 28, 1965.

Concrete foundations were dug sixty feet below ground, half of which were in bedrock.

The stainless steel exterior of the Arch is a quarter-inch thick and covers reinforced concrete for the first three hundred feet of each leg and carbon steel and rebar thereafter. The Arch used more steel than any other structure in history: nine hundred tons.

The Arch is made of stainless steel equilateral triangle sections, which gradually decrease in size. The base sections measure fifty-four feet per side and are twelve feet high. The legs are hollow, which allows for gondola-like elevators to haul visitors to the observation deck at the top. The ride in the five-person pod lasts only two minutes, which is quicker than taking the 1,076 steps.

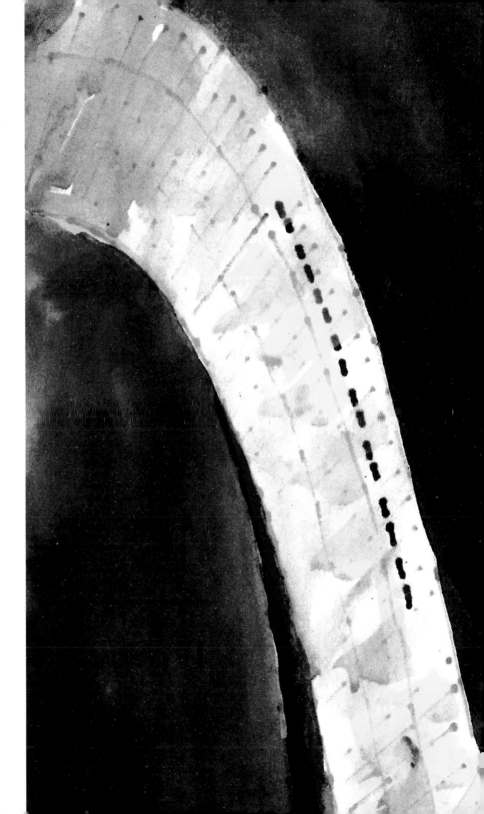

Bibliography

Fourth Exhibition of the St. Louis Architectural Club, catalog, 1913.

John Albury Bryan, *Missouri's Contribution to American Architecture.* St. Louis: St. Louis Architectural Club, 1928.

Elinor Martineau Coyle, *Saint Louis: Portrait of a River City.* St. Louis: The Folkestone Press, 1966.

Donald Dosch, *The Old Courthouse.* St. Louis: Jefferson National Expansion Memorial, 1979.

William Faherty, *The Saint Louis Portrait.* Tulsa: Continental Heritage, 1978.

William Barnaby Faherty, S. J., *St. Louis: A Concise History.* St. Louis: Convention and Visitors Bureau, 1990.

Gregory Franzwa, *The Old Cathedral.* St. Louis: Archdiocese of St. Louis, 1965.

Harry Hagen, *This Is Our Saint Louis.* St. Louis: Knight Publishing, 1970.

Ernest Kirschten, *Catfish and Crystal.* New York: Doubleday, 1960.

Selwyn Troen & Glen Holt, *St. Louis.* New York: New Viewpoints, 1977.

Koil Rowland, "This Is St. Louis, " in *Missouri Life,* 1979.

George McCue, *The Building Art in St. Louis.* American Institute of Architects, 1981.

Norris Smith, *The Architectural Heritage of St. Louis,* 1982.

Marilynne Bradley, *Borrowed Ideas and Famous Firsts,* 1984.

Robert Hannon, *St. Louis: Its Neighborhoods and Neighbors.* St. Louis: Regional Commerce and Growth Association, 1986.

Patti Smith Jackson, *The St. Louis Arena Memories.* St. Louis GHB Publishers, 2000.

Carolyn H. Toft, *St. Louis Landmarks and Historic Districts.* St. Louis: Landmarks Association of St. Louis, 1988.

Diane Rademacher, *Still Shining.* St. Louis: Virginia, 2003.

Carol Grove, *Henry Shaw's Victorian Landscapes: The Missouri Botanical Garden and Tower Grove Park.* University of Massachusetts Press, 2005.

Lou Ellen McGinley with Stephanie Spurr, *Honk for Service: A Man, a Tray and the Glory Days of the Drive-In.* Tray Days Publishing, 2004.

Shellee Graham, *Coral Court Motel, 1941–1995.* St. Louis: Virginia Publishing, 2000.

Mary Bartley, *St. Louis Lost: Uncovering the City's Lost Architectural Treasures.* St. Louis: Virginia Publishing, 1994.

History: Physical Growth of the City of St. Louis. St. Louis City Plan Commission, 1969.

Mary Bagley, *The Front Row: Missouri's Grand Theatres.* St. Louis: Gateway Publishing, 1984.

Ron (Johnny Rabbitt) Elz, *The Johnny Rabbitt St. Louis Trivia Game.* St. Louis: Virginia Publishing, 2006.

James Neal Primm, *Lion of the Valley.* St. Louis: Missouri Historical Press, 1998.

Charles Van Ravenswaay, *Saint Louis: An Informal History of the City and its People, 1764–1865.* St. Louis: Missouri Historical Press, 1991.

Women's Architectural League, *Architecture in St. Louis,* 1969.